AFGHANISTAN AND CHECHNYA:
Low Intensity Preludes To Another Revolution

Chapter 1: The Repetition of History?

> The world's attention span has been reckoned at 90 days, which, unhappily, is probably right. Afghanistan has all but slipped from sight...But the war still goes on. The Russians, incredibly, are no nearer victory than at the start, when experts blandly forecast that their modern army would subdue the primitive tribesmen in months. It is bigger news than a bored world realizes.
>
> *New York Times* editorial, 1 June 1982

I

For ten years, the Russians attempted to increase their influence in an area beyond their traditional borders. Only after a sound military defeat, did they acquiesce and humbly withdraw from the region. The defeat had tremendous social, political, economic and military repercussions at home. Within a year of this defeat, there was an uprising in Moscow. The people revolted to protest government inefficiency. The uprising was quelled, but political and social unrest persisted and flourished within Russia during the next eight years. In this period, sporadic revolts within the country were forcibly suppressed by the Russian Army. Yet, the military was becoming ineffective. It "...suffered from severe shortages of material and munitions. Its high command...was careless and incompetent..."[1] as they allowed the Russian Army and Navy to collapse.

One might interpret these events as an accurate description of recent Soviet history. While this may be so, the events described actually occurred nearly a century ago. They reflect a Russian historical chronology that began in 1895 with the occupation of Korea and Manchuria and later included the Russo-Japanese War in 1905. The chain of events eventually culminated in the Russian Revolution of 1917. If history repeats itself, the current conventional interpretation of Russian events is absolutely incorrect. The recent democratic revolution will not prevail as the new Russian order for the 21st Century. Rather, the Afghanistan and Chechen conflicts represent the beginning of another great Russian transformation. In fact, they may be considered low intensity preludes to the next high intensity revolution or possibly part of a wider Eurasian conflict with global implications!

In one sense, it is ironic that this century closes much as it began. A century ago, Russian leaders attempted to expand the empire. Their failure generated two decades of national turmoil that prompted a new totalitarian order which in turn, greatly defined much of the 20th Century global order. The recent Communist collapse presents current Russian leaders with similar political and economic choices that were faced eight decades ago. Once again the country is in turmoil and the pending decisions have the potential to mold the global order well into the next century.

In another sense, however, the dawn of the 21st century is dramatically different from its predecessor. The new world order includes unprecedented Asian economic and military might, a more uncertain balance between aggressive Islamic power structures, and a new coalition of European states attempting to peacefully redefine their identity. In the very center of these changes--where Asia, the Middle East and Europe converge--lies the great Russian landmass. Given the nature of these current global circumstances, the impact of Russia's decisions could have an opposite relationship (with regard to the 1917 revolution) on the sequence of the next Russian transformation. In other words, the relationship between wider global conflict and low intensity conflict (LIC) may be reversed. In the beginning of the 20th century, World War I served as a catalyst that magnified the effects of Russian LIC.

This research suggests that a LIC catalyst will precipitate the next Russian Revolution which has the potential to spread into a global or at least a multinational Eurasian conflict.

This thesis maintains that Russian LIC experiences in Afghanistan and Chechnya have accelerated dynamic conditions that are contributors to both the demise of the USSR and the detriment of the new Russian state. These LIC experiences have negatively affected Russian civil-military relations and the ability to formulate an effective national military doctrine. The current conditions generate increased LIC potential that may precipitate wider conflict in the future. Even though it is 14 years old, the introductory quote still retains two fundamental truths; the war in Russia still goes on and "it is truly bigger news than a bored world realizes.

The significance of these conditions should demand unparalleled attention, yet they do not. Many world leaders appear to be content with the end of the Cold War as they search for elusive peace dividends. This study has two major purposes. Hopefully, it will raise new questions concerning the role of LIC in the new world order of the 21st Century. More directly, it is intended to raise the level of awareness concerning major conflict potential on the Eurasian continent as a result of a Russian LIC catalyst. While the Cold War may be over, the potential for conflict with or between former Soviet forces has never been greater.

This study begins with a synopsis of the current Russian situation and supporting framework. The introduction does not include a detailed historical overview; it is designed only as a background for the thesis. A subsequent analysis of the Afghanistan and Chechen LIC experiences provides the framework for the main focus of this study--the LIC effect on Russian civil-military relations and national military doctrine. The study of recent political-military interactions will provide insight to the future of the transformation process and its interaction with the people. LIC is only one form of war, and its nature is similar to other forms of war, this analysis may thus follow a Clausewitzian foundation. The study will evaluate the Russian LIC experiences in relation to the "paradoxical trinity--composed of...the people...the commander and his army... [and] the government."[2] The conclusions will focus on the effects of prolonged LIC in relation to both the Russian trinity and the global powers in the new world order.

II

In a global context, all of the states that comprise the former Soviet Union (FSU) are facing two overwhelming challenges. First, these countries, along with the other members of the global community, find themselves awash in a rapidly changing international environment that equates to the new world order. Technological advances, increasingly interdependent economies and the rapidly changing character of war are only a few of the challenges that will revolutionize international relations in the next century. The newly independent states of the FSU, however, have not fully begun to deal with this new world order. Instead, they are mostly concerned with another challenge--forging a new national identity and infrastructure to replace decades of Communist domination. They are focused inward in a struggle to proliferate new freedoms and they are driven to enhance their future. For many, this future holds a promise that was incomprehensible just five years ago. Any event or force that might diminish these hopes and dreams will be met with tremendous resistance.

Russia, however, has a more complicated perspective as it attempts to deal with the new world order. The Russian transformation is unique when compared to other national transformations in the 20th Century. Japan and Germany, in the post World War II era provide the closest comparisons, yet they were dramatically different. A noted author on

Russian affairs, Daniel Yergin, explains that,

> Unlike Japan and Germany...the former Soviet Union is not a defeated country. The old factories still stand. While new people are entering the lists of power, many of the rulers of yesterday are still present today...although the ideology of Communism is gone, the mind-set of socialism is still very much alive. Defeat in war sometimes enables people to bury the past and start anew. But that option is not open to the Russians...*The past is still very much in place.*[3]

The complete Russian transformation is really comprised of three smaller transitions.[4]

The first transition focuses on the government and political structures' difficult move from

dictatorship to democracy. The military structure must deal with the political changes and

grapple with its role in democracy. More importantly, the military must fit into the second

transition from an empire to a nation-state. The third transition presents the greatest hurdle as

it affects the entire trinity; the ability to move from a controlled economy to a successful free

market economy may very well decide the future of the transformation.

The future political transition is set against a background of the void left by

Communism, new perspectives on constitutional guarantees and a dubious succession of

Russian leadership. The Communist Party of the Soviet Union (CPSU) served as the center

of power for the Communist ideology. Gorbachev's reforms initiated the political transition

that continues today. Much of the difficulty in this transition emanates from Gorbachev's

political deficits--as he weakened the CPSU, he failed to produce a viable political structure

that could replace it. It is important to understand that the maintenance "...of the Soviet

empire was supported by three central pillars: ideology, dictatorship and nationalism."[5] As

long as the ideology and the dictatorship were supported by a viable economy, the political

structure could control the nationalist sentiments. The constitution of the F SU guaranteed the independence of the constituent republics, but the dictatorship ensured that this guarantee would not be fulfilled. Once the dictatorship and ideology vanished, the only remaining pillar was nationalism. Without the other two pillars, the focus of nationalism rapidly changed as independence became the ultimate objective.

The rapid succession of Russian leaders during the past 14 years has also played a significant role in the political transition. Basic analysis supports a definitive correlation between weakened leadership and the FSU's entrance into prolonged LIC engagements. The first 65 years of the Communist Empire were ruled by just four leaders. Since the invasion of Afghanistan in December 1979, a period of 16 years, the Russians have been subject to no less than five leaders, and most were routinely afflicted by significant health problems that raised questions about their leadership ability. Whereas democracies are comfortable with frequent and peaceful transfers of political power, there is obviously no parallel for dictatorships. The two recent coup attempts serve as a bold reminder that "the past is still very much in place." The decision to use force in Chechnya raises significant doubt concerning the progress toward democracy. It also prompts more important questions: What happens when Russia faces the next LIC threat? Will the "needs" of the state outweigh the need to pursue democratic ideals? Will the leaders revert back "to the past" with which they are more comfortable?

The transition from empire to nation-state continues to have the greatest effect on the military. The former Soviet Army is in complete disarray. It has been unable to respond to the challenges of dynamic political change, ethnic fragmentation and the loss of prestige after two prolonged LIC engagements that failed to produce victory.

Three decades of Cold War posturing and the dictatorship's stability provided the military with a solid, well-defined foundation. In the late 1 970s, this foundation began to crack. Breshnev's ailing health, the subsequent succession crises and Gorbachev's political reforms changed the political landscape while the military was focused in Afghanistan. As the military attempted to heal the LIC imposed wounds, it found that its mission had changed; the Cold War was over. The modern Soviet Army was built, trained and oriented on defeating an external capitalist enemy. It was not prepared to assume a role as a decisive force in domestic politics. Military paralysis ensued as the empire crumbled from within and the military institution fragmented along ethnic lines.

The current military situation in Russia makes for an extremely unstable national condition. As the empire retreated from Eastern Europe and overseas bases, the returning military forces became outcasts in their own country. It is estimated that "as many as 150,000 Russian officers are currently homeless."[6] Many more have not been paid for extended periods. The Marshal of Aviation, Yevgeny Shaposhnikov, expressed his concerns as early as 1992 when he publicly revealed that "military capabilities had suffered 'severe damage' ...small arms were being stolen, and military assets were being proffered for self-- enrichment...It is little wonder that draft-dodging and desertion are rife...You've got the chaos and the civil-war is coming."[7] The problem has increased since the Chechen humiliation, which magnified the military's loss of status and prestige.

There is no doubt that some will dismiss this study's prediction of a pending violent revolution and potentially wider conflict (to include global scale) as being overly pessimistic or beyond reason. While the future may provide a peaceful Russian transformation, other factors must be also considered. The world is currently witnessing the end of over three and a half centuries of Russian expansion. In addition, the current Russian military leaders were raised and trained under the Brezhnev Doctrine which declared that no socialist government would be allowed to fail. What if sufficient military leaders opt to return to the past and attempt to rebuild the empire? Most of the current analysis agrees that the present Russian military is too fragmented to stage a successful conventional coup. Yet, what if one (or more) of the military assets that were stolen or proffered for self-enrichment included nuclear weaponry? The transition from empire to nation-state has created ample opportunities for further LIC proliferation within the FSU. More importantly, however, an attempt to reclaim the empire has the potential to also include global actors.

The third transition provides the foundation for the complete Russian transformation. The government, the military and the people are all dependent on the emergence of a healthy and free market economy. The economic history is best described by Gorbachev's 1986 address to the 27th Communist Party Congress. He stated that,

> Difficulties began to build up in the economy in the 1970s, with rates of economic growth declining visibly...Though efforts have been made of late, we have not succeeded in fully remedying the situation...Acceleration of the country's socio-economic development is the key to all our problems; immediate and long-term, economic and social, political and ideological, internal and external.[8]

In his 1989 book, Paul Kennedy correctly analyzed the Soviet economic future. His analysis revealed that "...the Soviet Union will face an economic crunch far more severe than anything encountered in the 1960s and 1970s."[9] Kennedy's only error was that he underestimated the effect of the predicted economic failure. He believed that the pending economic crunch did "...not mean that the USSR was close to collapse."[10] Both the Cold War and the LIC misadventures created a greater economic burden than even the best experts could have anticipated. The economic drain of the Cold War is well documented, however, the real costs of Soviet LIC involvement are just coming to light and merit closer attention. The parts of the extended Soviet empire that consumed the bulk of the LIC expenditures included: Mongolia, North Korea, Cuba, Vietnam, Afghanistan, Syria, Iraq, Angola, Ethiopia, South Yemen, Nicaragua and Grenada. It is estimated that "at least $40 billion was expended to support this empire since the early 1960s."[11]

Recent economic data reveals that the Russian economy is not making the required transition. In fact, the official gross national product (GNP) has declined by 40 percent between 1990 and 1995.[12] The Chechen conflict and other potential LIC engagements threaten to further overextend the Russian economy. Once again, if history serves as a guide to Russia's future, the potential for wider conflict is inevitable. Kennedy reinforces this view by revealing that,

> ...historically, *none* of the overextended, multinational empires--the Ottoman, the Spanish, the Napoleonic, the British--ever retreated to their own ethnic base until they had been defeated in a Great Power war, or...were so weakened by war that an imperial withdrawal was politically unavoidable...such transformations normally occur at very great cost, and not always in a predictable fashion.[13]

Under the current political, military and economic circumstances, there is little indication that the cost of the Russian transformation will be unique in history. When compared to previous empires, the Russian LIC experiences have been relatively inexpensive. Unless Kennedy has made a second error (in this case, one of *overestimation* of the transformation costs), the Russian transformation has only just begun, An attempt to understand the full impact of LIC on the Russian transformation process is essential. The new world order in the 21st century will be shaped by Russia's political, military and economic successes and failures in the LIC arena.

Chapter 2: The Low Intensity Preludes: Afghanistan And Chechnya

> Approach as near as possible to Constantinople and India. Whoever governs there will be the true sovereign of the world. Consequently, excite continual wars in Persia... penetrate as far as the Persian Gulf...advance as far as India.
>
> Peter the Great, 1775

> If victory is long in coming, the men's weapons will be dulled and their ardour dampened. If the campaign is protracted, the resources of the state will not be equal to the strain.
>
> Sun Tm, 400 B.C.

I

While the FSU has been involved in numerous LIC environments since the 1 960s, a detailed review of each is beyond the scope of this work. This paper only addresses the Russian LIC involvement in Afghanistan and Chechnya. The analysis of these conflicts will focus on two specific aspects: why these conflicts were initiated and their major impact on the Russian trinity. This method facilitates conclusions concerning future Russian LIC involvement and the future of the nation. In many ways, Afghanistan represents the transition from the Soviet past and Chechnya presents a view of the future.

Using historical tradition, Russian tsars and Soviet leaders considered Afghanistan as part of the empire. As such, they intervened in the region on a limited scale on three separate occasions in 1885, 1928 and 1930. A major invasion, however, was never attempted until 1979. Why then, after centuries of a relatively peaceful coexistence, did Soviet leaders decide to invade the country? The answer to this question assumes greater relevance considering that this was the first time since World War II the Soviet ground forces engaged in combat outside of the Warsaw Pact area. What motivated the Soviet leadership to venture beyond normal Cold War boundaries and invade Afghanistan?

Since 1979, there has been great speculation on the causes of the Soviet invasion. These speculations can be basically categorized as either offensively or defensively motivated. The defensive motivations have included: preventing the failure of a socialist regime (the Brezhnev Doctrine), the perceived threat of the effect of Islamic resurgence on 40 million Soviet Moslems, and the traditional fear of encirclement by non-Communist governments. The offensive motivations have included: the historical desire to gain a warm water port, the Soviet Union's desire to attain a better political position vis-à-vis the US. in the Middle East, and a need to enhance its strategic buffer between Pakistan and China.

While it is not feasible to completely separate the potential offensive and defensive motivations, the majority of the evidence suggests that the Soviet invasion was not defensively oriented.[14] This analysis concludes that in 1979 the world situation and the deteriorating Afghani domestic political situation combined to provide (what appeared to be) a relatively easy opportunity to exploit offensively motivated expansionist aims. The global events outside Afghanistan also intensified Moscow's offensive aspirations. Soviet geopolitical interests in the Middle East had steadily grown since World War II. By late 1978, the USSR enjoyed a fairly favorable situation in the region. The U.S. had imposed a Turkish arms embargo as a result of their actions in Cyprus. The U.S. was at odds with Pakistan over human rights and nuclear program violations. In Iran, the Shah had been deposed in the wake of an anti-American revolution. And finally, Afghanistan appeared to be conforming to Moscow's desires.

This favorable situation, however, rapidly deteriorated in 1979. The U.S. began to project its military strength into the Middle East as a result of the Iranian crisis. In March, Soviet-Iranian relations began to falter. Iran was charged with complicity in the Herat massacre where 50 to 100 Soviet advisors were killed. In April, Soviet fears were compounded by a perceived realignment in U.S., Chinese and Soviet relationships. The Chinese refused to renew a 1950 Sino-Soviet Treaty of Friendship, Alliance and Mutual Assistance and the U.S. was proposing to grant China the most-favored-nation status. Soviet fears were "confirmed" by what appeared to be aggressive U.S. actions which included: increased military budgets, the formation of the Rapid Deployment Force, the refusal to ratify SALT II agreements, and increased discussion of Pershing II and cruise missile deployments in Europe. The Soviets perceived that an offensive military thrust into Afghanistan might enhance their political position and strengthen their future geopolitical influence.

This research also identifies two other factors that influenced the invasion decision: the absence of constraints and historical misapplication. Although they are not categorized as either offensive or defensive, they did magnify existing offensive motivations. The Soviet leaders perceived an opportunity to undertake offensive military operations that would face relatively few external or internal constraints. The U.S. was distracted in Iran. Pakistan did not possess the will or the military power to deter the Soviets. In December, the Wakham Corridor that connects China with greater Afghanistan was impassable. The Afghan Army was politically divided and Soviet advisors controlled their logistical structure. The Politburo became mistakenly convinced that the invasion would be "...a low-cost operation, using less than 4 percent of the total ground forces, and, using Czechoslovakia as a guide...the complete occupation of key areas...would not take more than a few months."[15]

The misapplication of historical lessons also enticed the Russian leadership to proceed under false assumptions. This appears to be an extremely important and recurring factor in modern Russian LIC engagements. The explanation for the Soviet miscalculation in Afghanistan (as well as military miscalculations by other countries) is the attempt to selectively apply history in order to fit the present situation. Robert Jervis describes this phenomenon by stating that,

> When a policy has brought notable success, actors are likely to apply it to a range of later situations. But when insufficient attention is paid to the reasons why the policy worked in the past, the new situation will not be scrutinized to see if it has the same attributes that made the earlier success possible. Because the actor is apt to overestimate the degree to which his policy was responsible for the earlier success, he will be especially insensitive to the variation of the situation. Nothing fails like success.[16]

Afghanistan represents a significant LIC transition period for the USSR. The 1979 invasion was patterned after previous successful interventions in East Germany, Hungary and, especially, Czechoslovakia. In Afghanistan, as with the previous interventions, the Soviet Union was "pro-actively" preserving and strengthening the empire. In the European scenarios, the Kremlin provided a strong and focused national strategy that ensured success. Control of the cities in Europe meant political control. The leadership, however, failed to realize that the same conditions did not apply to a less developed country like Afghanistan. As the war became prolonged, Moscow was forced to adopt a defensive orientation that was aimed at producing acceptable terms for the eventual withdrawal of military forces. The dynamic conditions within the Soviet Union prevented the implementation of a focused national strategy. Over time, Afghanistan produced much broader ramifications throughout the USSR. It eventually "...exposed the very weakness of the military as well as the Soviet political structure and society itself."[17] The 1979 invasion represents the culminating point of the Soviet military and the empire. In Afghanistan, Soviet national strategy and traditional offensive military doctrine shaped the LIC involvement. All subsequent Russian LIC engagements have shaped a more defensive national strategy.

In order to accurately ascertain the effect of LIC, it is insufficient to simply proclaim that the Russian defeat in Afghanistan precipitated the demise of the empire. The Afghan LIC experience must be analyzed with respect to scope and the resulting effect on the government, the people and the military.

Since Afghanistan represents a significant Soviet transition, it is difficult to keep the scope of the war in perspective. On one hand, the war was monumental; it was a prelude to ruin. The war has been described as an experience that "...began as yet another step in the expansion of Soviet power ended in a welter of systematic institutional self doubt that exposed the corruption within the Soviet system and ultimately brought its parent state to ruin."[18] Conversely, when compared to other wars of similar duration, it was a relatively limited engagement. During the ten year war, Soviet troop strength in Afghanistan only averaged about 100,000 men. In comparison to Vietnam, where U.S. troop strength grew to over 500,000, the Soviet effort was significantly smaller. The number of missing and dead also illustrates the relatively limited scope of the war. In Afghanistan, 13,310 Soviet soldiers were killed as compared to the more than 58,000 in Vietnam. Other Russian "...losses included 118 jets, 333 helicopters, 147 tanks, 1,314 armored personnel carriers, 433 artillery pieces or mortars..." and over 13,000 vehicles.[19] While these losses represent significant

amounts of hardware, they were also a minuscule portion of the Soviet military inventory.

The real impact of Afghanistan was not the scope of the defeat in terms of military assets.

Instead, the significance of this LIC involvement must be measured according to the fallout

at home in terms of the government, the society and the military. In this sense, Afghanistan

and Vietnam were very similar and their lessons will be applicable in the 21st Century. The

impact of a LIC failure for major world powers will be disproportionately magnified in

relation to the military losses.

The Kremlin was unprepared to deal with a military defeat and withdrawal. The

leadership's reaction made the government structure even more susceptible to a

disproportionate LIC effect. The withdrawal represented a historic event that had not been

part of the Soviet experience for over three decades. It was the first time that the Soviets had

.voluntarily abandoned territory...since it withdrew from Austria after World War II in

1955..."[20] The Afghan failure also placed the government in an ideological dilemma for

which it was unprepared. The "Marxist-Leninist dogma did not allow for a 'war of national

liberation' where the people would fight against a Marxist regime."[21] As a result, the

dictatorship felt compelled to suppress the truth. After four years of war, "...the Soviet press

had only reported six dead and wounded soldiers..." while in reality the number actually

exceeded 16,000 killed and wounded.[22] By 1988, when *glastnost* allowed more accurate

media reporting, there was no choice but to face the situation and withdraw. Even though it

was a limited conflict, it, irreparably damaged the ideological, dictatorial and nationalistic

pillars of the empire.

The impact of the war on Soviet society was delayed, but in the end it was no less dramatic. During the war, the lack of media coverage forced the public to rely on returning troops for information. It was not the relatively low number of deaths that affected society; it was the survivors who revealed the grim truths. Of the 642,000 soldiers who served in Afghanistan, nearly 470,000 (73 percent of the force) fell victim to wounds, disease or serious illnesses.[23] As the domestic economy faltered, Soviet citizens "...did not understand why their sons were being conscripted for battle in a strange land and failed to see how their sacrifices contributed to the security of the fatherland."[24] In most LIC engagements, the significant societal effects are reduced once the conflict ends. In the USSR, however, the effects increased *after* the war and they are still very much present in the FSU today. This phenomenon reinforces the idea that the transition that began in the Afghan mountains has not yet ended.

The reason for this effect on Russian society lies in the ethnic composition of the FSU. While resurgent Islamic fundamentalism was not a major Soviet concern in 1979, the Afghan experience may create greater problems in the future. The Soviet withdrawal precipitated a civil war between rival Afghan factions. This conflict continues on less secure Russian borders and threatens to increase regional instability in former Soviet republics like Tajikistan and Azerbaijan. The breakup of the Soviet Union left 25 million Russians outside of Russia's territory. If a segment of this population becomes threatened or involved in a new LIC environment, the ethnic Russian population may intervene within or across new borders in order to protect fellow citizens.

The specific effects of Afghanistan and the LIC environment on the Russian military will be addressed in greater detail in subsequent chapters. It must be noted, however, that the Afghan War has left both negative and positive effects on the Russian military. In the negative sense, the loss of prestige and status caused by Afghanistan and the demise of the dictatorship, still plagues the Russian military today. For the first time,

> ...the returning soldiers were not welcomed as heroes or treated with respect. They were shunned and often scorned by their fellow citizens. A gap opened between the Armed Forces and the citizenry and many veterans found they could not fit back into the lifestyle of the complacent and self-centered citizenry.[25]

The Afghan War marked the beginning of a dangerous military transition that continues today. The source of military power has become increasingly isolated from not only the government, but more importantly, from the people. Afghanistan unbalanced the Russian trinity.

In a positive sense, however, the Afghan War forced Russian political and military leaders to change their military from a Cold War structure well before the Cold War ended. Given the current international situation, the Russian military will most likely face numerous LIC threats in the new world order. If applied, lessons learned as a result of the Afghan War can certainly be valuable in the future. Lester Grau's book, *The Bear Went Over the Mountain,* is one source that demonstrates that the Russians are attempting to learn from past mistakes.[26] With the exception of the Russian nuclear threat, Western observers appear to disregard the latent potential of a country that was a military superpower only a few years ago. In war, combat experience is a significant force multiplier. The West should not forget that the Russian military has been engaged in LIC during 12 of the past 17 years. The

Russian military has more recent and in-depth LIC combat experience than any other major military in the world.

These positive effects must not be overstated. The status of the current Russian military is certainly very low. In addition, as the years pass, the combat experience factor will decay. During the next few years, however, the possibility exists for the resurrection of a significant military force. Given the right circumstances and opportunities, the Russian military has the potential to significantly affect the new world order. The lessons of Afghanistan may reappear when they are least expected.

II

On the 12th anniversary of the Afghan invasion, Mikhail Gorbachev announced on television: "I hereby discontinue my activities at the post of president of the Union of Soviet Socialist Republics..."[27] With this announcement, "...the red flag with hammer and sickle...was lowered, and the white-blue-and-red flag of the Russian federation rose in its place."[28] This event represented a significant step in the transformation of the old empire. It occurred just three years after the complete withdrawal from Afghanistan. Future events, however, would reveal that the transformation was in jeopardy. Within three years, the military would again be fighting on the periphery of the country. The invasion of Chechnya represents a significant step backwards in the pursuit of a new Russian order as the deputy editor-in-chief of the *Moscow News* revealed: Chechnya "is not the irony of history, but its vengeance: the Russian president marked the first anniversary of the Russian Constitution with the bombardment of Russian inhabited localities and a tank parade in the republics of the Northern Caucasus."[29] The new democracy attempted to resolve an old problem with old methods.

Russian influence in the Caucasus region dates back to the reign of Ivan the Terrible in the 16th Century. They intervened again in the late 18th Century, the 1860s, the 1940s and in 1957. In order to understand the current situation, a complete review of the historical involvement is not required; a general appreciation of the temperament of the area is sufficient. The Northern Caucasus region is noted for prolonged instability and its people have a reputation for being ruthless and fiercely determined. One source explains that with the Chechen history "...the present war is no mystery; it is the 37 years of peace from 1957 to 1994 that are an enigma."[30] Even considering this tumultuous history, it is difficult to understand why an invasion was mandated in 1994. After all, the Russian empire was dismantled into 15 separate states; independence was granted routinely throughout much of the FSU. Why was Chechnya different? The Northern Caucasus (of which Chechnya only occupies a small part) comprises less than one percent of the Russian landmass and it contains less than 1.5 million people. With numerous challenges facing the new democracy, why was it so important to fight for a very small and extremely volatile region?

The official reason for the invasion was proclaimed by President Yeltsin on 11 December 1994. He stated that the situation constituted

> ...a threat to the integrity of Russia and to the safety of its citizens both in Chechnya and beyond its boundaries, and by the possibility of a destabilization of the political and economic situation. Our objective is to find a political solution to the problems of one of the subjects of the Russian Federation--the Chechen Republic--and to protect its citizens against extremism.[31]

This analysis suggests that domestic political power struggles in Moscow provided the main impetus for the invasion. Economic considerations, apparent lack of constraints and historical miscalculation (similar to Afghanistan) also served as minor motivations to invade.

The preservation of Russian territorial boundaries was also a consideration: however, this factor served as a primary cover for alternative agendas.

While the preservation of Russian territory may have been a valid motivation, it should not be considered the primary objective. The Russian federal structure was very unstable between 1991 and 1993 as numerous republics declared independence. By 1994, Chechnya was the only republic failing to recognize a new constitutional basis for the federal structure. Yeltsin became concerned that unabated Chechen freedom may initiate a domino effect and reverse the recent constitutional gains. In other words, by 1994, "...Chechen independence became the exception rather than the rule--and was a major eyesore for a Russian President seeking to consolidate and strengthen state power."[32] For Yeltsin, the inability to consolidate and strengthen state power foreshadowed his failure to win the next election.

Michael McFaul has supported the domestic political power struggle theory by claiming that "...Yeltsin did not order his troops into Chechnya to save the Russian Federation--He moved against Chechnya to save his presidency."[33] After parliamentary elections in December 1993, Yeltsin became increasingly concerned about his reelection in 1996. Vladimir Zhirinovsky's Liberal Democratic Party was gaining surprising popularity. Zhirinovsky's "...extreme nationalist views, law-and-order rhetoric and racist undertones resonated with an electorate tired of both the communist past and the 'democratic' present."[34] Yeltsin became convinced that he needed to project a "get tough" persona and distance himself from the democratic leadership. Without some dramatic event to distract the public attention from the ailing economy, reelection hopes were rapidly disappearing. Chechnya presented a potential victory that could rally supporters. Or, if the situation was presented as a grave national threat, a state of national emergency might be "required" that could provide the justification for postponing future elections.

The primary economic consideration for the invasion was oil. Several major oil pipelines run between the Caspian Sea and the Black Sea--in between lies Chechnya. Russia successfully negotiated contracts with Western oil companies to use the Chechen pipeline rather than alternate routes through Georgia or Turkey. These contracts represented a sizable boost for a weak economy. If Chechnya was granted independence, then new pipelines would be required around Chechnya. This construction was too costly and did not present a viable option. The Chechens magnified the problem in June 1994 when they broke off oil licensing fee negotiations with Moscow. The economic bottom line ensured that Russian leaders would persistently pursue the control of oil shipments and the regional revenues.

In late summer, Russia attempted to reduce international constraints for an invasion. In August, Russian officials met with their U.S. counterparts and proposed to link Chechnya "...with America's projected invasion of Haiti by means of reciprocal endorsements at the UN"" At a subsequent summit in September, President Clinton expressed doubt about this linkage. One source reported that Yeltsin responded harshly by stating: "You watch your backyard and we'll watch ours." President Clinton's "...ensuing silence was taken as acknowledgment that Chechnya was Russia's internal affair and that Yeltsin could take whatever measures necessary to subdue it."[36]

Much like Afghanistan, the LIC environment in Chechnya appeared to present the Kremlin with the opportunity for a quick victory. Misapplication of history again created an opportunity for failure. In one case, "Yeltsin's advisors promised a quick victory much like the U.S. action in Haiti."[37] Even the Minister of Defense, Pavel Grachev, failed to appreciate the historical lessons of Chechen willpower and tenacity. In a press interview on 29 November, he claimed that Grozny could be captured with "one airborne regiment within two hours."[38] A quick little war would bolster his reputation. In addition, a successful military action would send a strong message to other republics and might preclude additional movements for independence.

With the invasion of Chechnya in December 1994, Russian leaders experienced the new future of the state. Unlike the Afghan invasion, where the national strategy and military doctrine shaped the LIC engagement, now the reverse was true. The political and military leaders were reacting defensively to preserve their personal power, the fragile constitution and the nation. Their failure diminished future prospects in all three areas.

Before analyzing the impact of Chechnya on the Russian trinity, a significant question must be addressed: Did either side win the war in Chechnya? The Chechen War, like most LIC engagements, produced far more losers than winners. The worst possible situation currently prevails in the region; neither opponent has really achieved its desired political ends. As such the war is not really over--it is a war without an end as both sides have agreed to postpone the final battles for a five year period.

While the Chechens may not have lost, their casualty figures hardly denote victory. Most sources estimate the Chechen death toll at 40,000, yet one report by the former National Security Chief. Alexander Lebed, recently revised the number upward to between 70,000 and 90,000.[39] The number of wounded ranges as high as 240,000 and the number of refugees has been placed at 487,000. These figures indicate that almost 60 percent of the population has been killed, wounded or displaced.

Contrary to Moscow's victory proclamations, the Russian casualty reports are not representative of a decisive military victory in the LIC environment. On 2 September 1996, the Russian Defense Minister, Igor Rodinov reported 2,837 soldiers killed, 337 missing and 13,270 wounded. Using these figures, table one reveals that the overall casualty rate per year is higher in Chechnya than in Afghanistan.

Even though it was shorter, Chechnya's impact is no less significant. In fact, Russian LIC appears to be taking an increasingly greater toll in terms of casualties.

Neither is Chechnya's impact on the Russian Government any less significant. Prior to the 1996 elections, the entire balance between Russian political factions was upset. The domestic political groups that had carefully gained popular support during the previous four to five years, "...suddenly lost meaning as the divide over the war took on greater saliency."[42] Not only was LIC shaping national military strategy and doctrine, it was now the predominant factor shaping the domestic political scene. Once again, Russian LIC had produced disproportionate effects within the country. Russian political leaders are learning LIC lessons that U.S. political leaders learned 20 years ago: Even the smallest LIC engagements have the potential to redefine national political support and unseat heads of state.

It is not surprising that Yeltsin signed a Chechen cease-fire peace agreement just three weeks prior to the election. Without this agreement, it is doubtful that he would have been reelected. Neither should it be a surprise that the cease-fire agreement was broken by Russian forces less than four weeks after the election. This fact raises an extremely important issue for future Russian LIC. If Russian leaders (either political or military) use LIC primarily for the enhancement of personal power, the democracy will be subject to an untenable relationship between political ends and military means. Russian leaders must begin to treat their relatively new LIC problems with new Russian methods or the transformation of the state will fail.

Unfortunately, recent events indicate that a genuine attempt to resolve the Chechen War is still subordinate to domestic political power struggles. The architect of a second peace deal, Alexander Lebed, was fired from his post as National Security Chief just six weeks after the agreement was signed. The Russian Prime Minister declared Lebed's accord illegal. In addition, the "... Interior Minister Anatoly Kulikov drew loud applause in the State Duma (lower house of Parliament) when he described the peace deal as a humiliating step towards the disintegration of Russia."[43] Political maneuvering in Moscow peaked in early November as Yeltsin entered the hospital for heart surgery. Once again the government is attempting to resolve a conflict while its leadership is physically incapacitated.

The unresolved Chechen conflict may be the LIC catalyst that precipitates the next Russian Revolution. In looking to the future, one must ask: Why were the negotiations delayed for five years? One answer reveals that this period allows President Yeltsin to complete his current four year term and keep his pledge of keeping Chechnya as part of Russia. One problem with the five year time frame is that the domestic political infighting will increase as the Chechen deadline awaits less than 12 months after the next election. By that time, it is possible that "...not all of the presidential contenders will be advocating the democratic process. After...years of 'democracy'--currently understood in Russia as anarchy, crime, poverty, and now civil war--voters may well be ready for a new order."[44] This analysis views this five year postponement as the worst possible solution. It provides a potentially explosive situation for the future.

The impact of the Chechen LIC experience on Soviet society revolves around the relationships with other republics and their ethnic undertones, and the impact of the media. This conflict has sent mixed signals to the people of other Russian republics. On the positive side, ethnic republic relations have become a top priority as the Russian Government seeks to avoid a similar experience. By "...the beginning of 1995, the Duma has debated and/or adopted at least 5 pieces of legislation on regional and nationalities issues."[45] This is a significant increase from previous years when the federal government was preoccupied with internal matters. In the aftermath of Chechnya, there has been increased support for a complete realignment of the pre-revolutionary Russian provinces. This proposed realignment is based on economic rather than ethnic boundaries. Given the historical ethnic basis of Russian territory, it is doubtful that the people would submit to, or recognize, these divisions.

In the negative sense, Chechnya demonstrated that "the government is more determined than ever to preserve the unity of the Russian Federation at all costs, even if it involves the use of military force."[46] More importantly, the Chechen conflict has sent conflicting signals to various factions within these republics and polarized the public opinion. On one side, Chechnya represents an end to future hopes of independence--where, regardless of public opinion, Russian military intervention will be mandated even if it means the destruction of a homeland. In other words, further attempts to gain greater freedoms are not worth the cost incurred by the Chechens. The other side sees an opportunity. They are no longer afraid of Russia and make the same assumption as Amir Akhmutov, the Chairman of Tartarstan's unofficial Committee for Sovereignty; they believe that "if it [Russia] failed to defeat tiny Chechnya, it won't be able to defeat such a big republic as Tartarstan."[47] If Russian economic problems continue to grow, it becomes increasing likely that more Russians will view the Chechen conflict as a precedent for opportunity.

The role of the media and its affect on Russian society is still unclear. In one sense, Chechnya was similar to Vietnam; it was Russia's first "television war." Just as it took the U.S. many years to fully appreciate the media's effect on society during a LIC engagement, Russia is currently learning similar lessons. Compared to the U.S., however, Russian society perceives the media in a vastly different light. Years of censorship and media control has left the public highly suspicious of what they are shown. On the other hand, the media from Chechnya also produced a sense of shock. For the first time, Russian society was viewing scenes that have become fairly routine for Western audiences in the past 25 to 30 years. Many Russian people felt uncomfortable "...seeing their forces engage in the terror bombing that ensued when ground forces failed to advance over land."[48] This media aspect may widen the gap between society and the military. The effect of the media in relation to all aspects of the trinity in Russian LIC is an area that provides significant opportunity for additional research.

In the analysis of Chechnya's effect on the Russian military, one important point must be remembered--the total effect of this LIC is on going. Russian LIC scholars must not analyze these types of interventions as isolated incidents. Recent Russian interventions are vastly different from their Soviet predecessors in Eastern Europe. Afghanistan initiated a new era and Chechnya represents another phase in a new Russian *process* of LIC interaction. In order to better understand this phenomenon, the remainder of this analysis examines the dynamic process of Russian LIC in relation to civil-military relations and military doctrine. The analysis seeks to provide insight into the civil-military relations process and its relation to future LIC as Russia attempts to balance the expansive dreams of Peter the Great and the warning of Sun Tzu.[49]

Chapter 3:
LIC And The Transformation Of Russian Civil-Military Relations

> Political power grows out of the barrel of a gun... Our
> principle is to have the party control the gun and never
> allow the gun to control the party.
> > Mao Tse-Tung, 1938

> Let us at long last recognize that so far we have a weak state
> and that there is no elementary order in the country.
> > Boris Yeltsin, Speech to the Durna,
> > 1994

I

This analysis examines Russian civil-military relations as they pertain to recent LIC

combat experiences in an effort to derive conclusions concerning Russia's future by using a

simple chronological methodology. The chronology is divided into three distinct phases; pre-

1980, 1980-1991, and 1992 to the present. Phase I provides a historical view of the

environment from which the current Russian leaders emerged. Phase II identifies significant

aspects of a remarkable transition period. Phase III addresses civil-military relations in the

new Russian state where the decline of the previous institutions of Communist order (the

Party and the military) have left an absence of elementary order. Only by understanding the

civil-military transformation process can a course for the future be identified.

The civil-military relations analysis becomes even more compelling when it is set

against a significant recurring theme in the history of Imperial Russia. Without exception, the

return of Russian troops from foreign wars was always associated with domestic turmoil,

upheaval and even revolution. A brief historical quote illustrates this point:

> The Decembrist uprising was led by young officers who had fought in the Napoleonic
> Wars and became disillusioned... The war in the Crimea encouraged the reforms of
> the 1860s... defeat in the Russo-Japanese War of 1905 precipitated revolutionary

upheavals...And as World War I dragged on...a profound war weariness helped make possible the October Revolution...[50]

II

From this history, the Red Army emerged. As a result, from 1918 to 1980, the Soviet civil-military relationship was a delicate balance between authoritarian political control and a vast military force. A survey of the historical Soviet civil-military relations literature reveals that Party-military interactions evolved through a cyclic pattern of tensions. The principle of Party control over the military was the primary factor in determining the amount of influence and the distribution of Soviet military power. To counter these controls, the military used both domestic and international crises situations to advance their institutional interests.

The communist leadership felt compelled to institute numerous oppressive measures to keep the military in its "proper" place. The use of these measures and the degree of repression fluctuated between the extremes of Stalin's purges to periods of relative tranquillity. These fluctuations were directly dependent on the political leader's requirement of military power in order to preserve and strengthen the Soviet fatherland. The use of commissars or political officers was the most prevalent method of control. The degree of Party control exercised by commissars also fluctuated. When Party-military tensions were relatively calm, the political officers were limited to an advisory role. When tensions were elevated, however, they were granted the power to veto the professional military decisions of commanding officers.

The most oppressive and destructive measure was Stalin's purges. He viewed the Soviet military as a greater threat to his regime than the opposing world powers. This control measure was not reduced until the Axis Powers were perceived as a greater threat.

Subsequent political leaders refrained from using such a destructive method. Instead, they used periodic personnel reductions, transfers, blackmail, selective career advancement and monetary privileges to ensure Party control over the "gun."

Throughout this period, Soviet military leaders actively resisted Party control measures and even possessed their own means to advance institutional interests. In 1953, military leaders began to manipulate domestic Soviet political alliances to win concessions from the Party. This tactic was especially effective during political succession crises. Dale Herspring noted, that "Khruschev relied heavily on the military between 1955 and 1957 in order to consolidate his power...and Brezhnev drew most of his support from the veteran party and military executives... "[51] Military leaders also used various other methods to counter the Party. The military never lost sight of the fact that an increase in military technology forced the political leaders to rely more on their expertise to meet the requirements of modern warfare. The military was also always on the ideological offensive. The military leaders continuously reminded the politicians that the armed forces were the protectors of the great socialist homeland and the communist system.

Even with these means of resistance, there are historical lessons that advise caution to the military's leadership in their role in the Russian political arena. The removal of Marshal Zhukov in 1957 serves as a vivid example of the consequences for deviating too far from the correct path.[52] Between 1954 and 1957, Marshal Zhukov, the Minister of Defense, systematically reduced political controls during a period of intense intra-Party struggles. By 1957, the Party leadership felt threatened and he was removed from office. Extremely strict Party controls were reintroduced which significantly undermined military discipline and proficiency. Political security prevailed over military efficiency.

As the Cold War progressed, the Soviet military assumed a wider mission that provided the initial introduction into the LIC environment. The first "massive extension" of Soviet military power outside of the Eurasian continent occurred in 1969-70 in the Suez Canal area. This intervention set the stage for a decade of Soviet foreign intervention. The USSR projected military power (to varying degrees) in the October War (1973), Angola (1975-6), the Ogaden War (1977-8) and finally in Afghanistan.[53] Throughout the decade, the military substantially increased its presence outside of the Warsaw Pact area. By 1977, they had 11,700 military advisors in Somalia and a similar build up in Vietnam was beginning. During this period, the Soviet military became more than the protector of the fatherland; it became a means of global expansion for the communist ideology. This expansion forced the military to deviate from its traditional role. Almost unwittingly, the political leadership thrust the military into a wider LIC environment without significant preparation, training or reorganization. The military achieved relative success in this dynamic situation until the realities of the Afghan War initiated a transition period in civil-military relations.

III

The civil-military tension cycle was relatively tranquil in phase II. There is little evidence to support any major political-military disagreement concerning the decision to invade Afghanistan. In many respects, it appears that the historical misapplications created a perception that the invasion was merely "business as usual." It is surprising, however, to find little evidence of civil-military tensions as the war met with repeated failures through the mid-1980s. This analysis finds several explanations for this phenomenon. First, it appears that a significant change occurred between 1983 and *1985.* The Afghan War was perceived to have "moved at least partly into the category of 'motherland defense.'"[54] As a result, Party controls were reduced as military proficiency assumed greater relative importance.

Another explanation is the high promotion rate for senior officers who served in Afghanistan. It appears that the political leadership promoted those with combat experience in an effort to motivate and improve the morale of the officer corps. This promotion pattern continued to the very end of the conflict. General Gromov, the last Soviet commander in Afghanistan, was given a prestigious military appointment on the same day he departed Afghanistan with the last Soviet troops. As a result, the military leaders preferred to remain outside of politics during the most turbulent series of succession crises in Soviet history.

Neither is there any evidence of political-military disagreements over the withdrawal decision. Even though the military welcomed the combat experience and the higher promotion rates, by 1988 they became concerned about a completely new aspect of Soviet society: public opinion. As previously addressed in Chapter Two, *glastnost,* more accurate media reporting and the returning wounded forced the leadership to face the situation. As society became increasingly polarized by the war, the military became aware of the detrimental effects of prolonging an increasingly unpopular LIC misadventure. A leading Russian civil-military relations expert, Timothy J. Colton, concluded that "... top civilian leadership and top military commanders of the Soviet Union stumbled into Afghanistan together, became mired down mutually, and decided jointly upon withdrawal."[55]

If the Afghan War did not greatly increase civil-military tensions or significantly alter historical Party-military relationships, how can this analysis justify phase II as a period of tremendous transition? This thesis supports the idea that the Afghan conflict was not a transition in and of itself. Rather, it served as the mechanism that allowed the recurring theme of Imperial Russia to revisit the Soviet State. The return of Russian troops from a foreign war again met with domestic turmoil and upheaval. Phase II culminated in the democratic revolution in 1991 as Mikhail Gorbachev resigned and the empire faded away.

The end of the Afghan War was not the only factor that led to the revolution, it merely magnified and accelerated other factors that contributed to the revolutionary process. As the conflict was terminating, a surge of nationalist movements erupted throughout the USSR. The multitude of events that occurred in 1988-1991 defy any attempt to analyze specific cause and effect relationships in civil-military relations. This research suggests that civil-military differences had less impact--relative to the broad changes in military doctrine--on the transition process between 1988 and 1991. There are, however, several key civil-military aspects of this phase that must be addressed.

Once the nationalist independence movements gained momentum, the political leadership was faced with a new dilemma never before witnessed in Soviet history. The use of military force to deter nationalistic movements became counterproductive to the interests of the state and jeopardized the power of the politicians. When the Brezhnev Doctrine died, the old Soviet civil-military relationship assumed opposite characteristics. No longer did the Party and the army rely on each other to preserve an ideology. Now the political leaders were forced to distance themselves from the use of military force. As independence and prosperity became the focus for the people, the economic well being—rather than the security—of the state garnered the attention of the political leadership. As a result, the military became a stepchild of both the government and society.

The traditional civil-military relationships began to erode between 1988 and 1991 as the military institution became isolated from the other two parts of the trinity. In much the same way that the empire crumbled from within, the military began to self destruct for several reasons. First, the economic and military reforms caused an unprecedented rise in interservice rivalries. Second, the forces of nationalism widened the gap between the predominately ethnic Russian officer corps and the enlisted troops, who were mostly non-Russian and tended to identify with their ethnic background. As a result, widespread "....violence occurred in many units, destroying cohesion, discipline and readiness."[56] Most importantly, when the military was tested in a series of domestic LIC engagements, the result

> ... had extremely corrosive effects on institutional discipline and self image. Beginning with attempts to use military units to put down disturbances in Tbilisi in 1989, followed by Baku in 1990, Vilnius in 1991, and ending with the failed coup of August 1991, the military establishment learned that institutional cohesion, discipline and political fortune always suffered in the aftermath of such activities.[57]

This "Tbilisi Syndrome" forced the military to shift allegiances. As the Communist ideology, the dictatorship and the empire dissolved under Gorbachev, the military was left without its historical basis. By 19 August 1991, there was only one perceived method of preserving the military establishment. The military allegiance had to shift to Boris Yeltsin and the new political leadership. A new phase in Russian civil-military relations was born.

IV

Phase III of Russian civil-military relations is unique in history. Rarely does a military establishment outlive its host institution in such a manner. The effects of the attempted coup on Russian civil-military relations were immediate. Less than a week after the attempted coup, the new Defense Minister "announced plans for a wholesale purge that...would replace 'about 80 percent of the top command structure with younger officers.'"[58] These purges strengthened the "Tbilisi Syndrome." Within four months, the military suffered complete paralysis. The military leadership quickly learned the best course of action in domestic LIC engagements was no action. The political leaders created an environment that turned the military into "...a concensual organization, where officers and units take direction from above on a case-by-case basis. They vote on whether to follow orders."[59]

The paralysis was caused by more than just the initial shuffling of the officer corps. By December, when the red flag adorned with the hammer and sickle was lowered for the last time, the military assumed a completely new role. It was no longer the defender of an ideology; in theory, it became the protector of the people. Both the political and military institutions were forced to reassess roles and relationships.

President Yeltsin used several methods of ensuring the military's abstention from direct political involvement. His policy toward the military was "consistently careful and respectful from the first... [he] reined back attempts to purge the officer corps...[60] He provided monetary compensation to limit the decline of their standard of living and allowed senior officers to publicly address political issues. And even when some senior officers began selling military equipment, Yeltsin would not permit investigations that might embarrass the military leadership.

It was not until 5 May 1992 that the military received formal guidance that would establish its new role. On this date, the Federation Law "On Security" was signed by Yeltsin. This law outlined the new concept of national security, the perceived threats to the state and a framework for the relationship between Russian and Commonwealth of Independent States (CIS) military forces. This law was a contrast "...to earlier Communist days, [when] the notion of security was anchored firmly to individual and national values."[61] It represented a new beginning that would face a severe test in less than 16 months.

Yeltsin's military policies yielded significant dividends in the Fall of 1993. As a second coup attempt threatened the new political order, the civilian leadership convinced the military to use force of arms to storm the Supreme Soviet. Most sources agree that the few military units that were used agreed to the use of force only after considerable debate. At this point, the political-military foundations and relationships were questionable. In order to enhance this relationship, Yeltsin continued to cater to the needs of the military. On 2 November 1993, he approved the draft "Provisions of the Military Doctrine of the Russian Federation." The timing of the approval provides great insight into the political-military interactions of the period. One source suggests that

> ...the timing of the release of the doctrine lends credence to suspicions that this was one of Yeltsin's 'payoffs' to the military for their 'support' during the crisis in October...a first draft...was published in May 1992 and was 'under discussion' since that time. General Staff officers repeatedly expressed their frustration that they could not get the doctrine approved by the government...It is interesting, then, that the first agenda item at the first Security Council meeting on October 6, after the crushing of the Parliamentary rebellion was the Military Doctrine.[62]

Chechnya was the next crisis that greatly affected the evolution of the civil-military process. Unlike Afghanistan, the decision to intervene in Chechnya did not achieve political-military consensus. In fact, the research indicates that many senior leaders in the Defense Ministry were not even aware of the decision to use force. This use of force represented a monumental step backward for Yeltsin's political career, civil-military harmony and the military institution. As already noted, Chechnya became a major hurdle in Yeltsin's bid for reelection. More importantly, it prompted considerable questions concerning his vision of democracy. In effect, Chechnya defied "...the 1992 Law on Defense, the army was used on the Russian population without any recourse to Parliament."[63] By all accounts, the invasion was illegal. This provided a basis for some senior officers to refuse to participate. Some evidence suggests the sole reason for the military decision to intervene was not in response to political direction. Instead, the military intervened only after Chechen forces attacked Russian military forces. In a sense, the military was no longer defending democracy or the political establishment; they were protecting themselves. The situation exacerbated the existing differences within the military institution and undermined the military's support for Yeltsin and the Minister of Defense, Grachev. By 1995, the LIC fallout had a disproportionate effect on both the civil-military interactions and the entire Russian state. One source identifies the gravity of the Chechen conflict by stating that

> This phenomenon not only underscores the pervasive lack of respect for Grachev and Yeltsin among the military, it also highlights the essential unreliability of the army when it comes to quelling domestic unrest. Efforts to impose such repression elsewhere could conceivably break the state apart...The Chechen operation, or other similar...ones, could, if protracted, lead to massive military disobedience on the scale of February 1917.[64]

The Chechen conflict quickly convinced military leaders that, as a divided institution, they did not possess the military resources to prevail in the current LIC environment. Nor did they possess the political resources to prevail in the political environment. This situation prompted the military to make an attempt to enhance its political base. In October 1995, Grachev "announced that the Ministry of Defense (MOD) was selecting and sponsoring 123 active duty and retired military men to run for office in the 17 December Duma elections."[65] This program represented a complete reversal of MOD policies in less than 24 months. Based on an understanding of the military's relative decline and overall situation in recent years, it is not too surprising that the institution turned to democracy rather than force of arms in a self preservation attempt. What is alarming, however, is the intensity of Grachev's program. He actually "summoned district commanders and senior generals and told them: 'I have never called on you to run for the Duma, but now I shall judge your service and performance by the number of deputies elected from the armed forces."[66]

By late 1996, Yeltsin had solidified his political situation. He successfully used Chechen cease-fire agreements to increase his chances of being reelected and he maneuvered a deal to postpone a final resolution for five years. With his successful reelection and the Chechen situation on hold, Yeltsin was able to consolidate his power base at the expense of the military leadership. Immediately after the election, Grachev was blamed for the Chechen failure and fired. His replacement was Igor Rodionov. Since October 1996, Rodionov has served as Yeltsin's hatchet-man; the systematic replacement of numerous general officers continues to this day.

What, then, lies ahead in terms of the Russian civil-military relations process? Will civil-military relations continue to evolve in a relatively peaceful cyclic pattern of political-military tensions? Perhaps a better question might be, when will some dramatic event completely transform the civil-military relationship and begin phase IV? This analysis suggests that phase IV is a matter of *when, not if.* In other words, the military will not accept the civil-military relations status quo when the next LIC involvement is mandated. This scenario is even more likely if the LIC is used by the politicians to enhance their own power base at the expense of the people or the military. All three parts of the trinity must play a crucial role for the transformation of the Russian state to succeed. For the military, only a few choices exist. They can either support, join, ignore or interrupt the democratic process. So far, in phase III, they have attempted to support, ignore and join the process. These methods have met with very limited success. The military establishment continues its declining spiral relative to relations with society, the government and its historical past. By process of elimination, there is probably only one alternative for the future: an interruption of the process. This analysis believes that when this alternative is pursued, the military or decisive military action will precipitate a revolution in civil-military relations. The exact nature of phase IV cannot be determined. However, there is little doubt that the military will be inextricably involved in the attempt to reestablish elementary order in the country.

Chapter 4: The Changing Perspectives of Russian Military Doctrine

> Between our proletarian state and the rest of the bourgeois world there can only be one condition--that of long, persistent, desperate war to the death...The common, parallel existence of our proletarian Soviet state with the states of the bourgeois world for a protracted period is impossible.
> Mikhail V. Frunze, Russian Civil War Hero, 1921

> The main danger to stability and peace is posed by local wars and armed conflicts. The likelihood of their arising in certain regions is growing; most notably in the regions to the south of Russia.
> 1992 Russian Draft Military Doctrine

I

The demise of the Soviet empire has profoundly affected the national military doctrine. The LIC experiences were integral factors that shaped the Russian military doctrine transition process after the mid-1980s. This process began slowly and quietly in the mountains of Afghanistan as Soviet forces met with repeated failures. It assumed global implications when Gorbachev instituted his reforms. The disintegration of the empire mandated further changes to meet the challenges of a post Cold War world. In this new atmosphere of "peace and independence," Chechnya confirmed the weakness of the Russian military doctrine.

This chapter addresses the two fundamental aspects of Russian national military doctrine. In just over ten years, the Russian military establishment was forced to change from a global superpower perspective to a new perspective that was founded on national self-preservation. Rather than looking outward to shape the world, it now looks inward to save itself and the fragile democracy. The second aspect deals with inability of the military to deal with the dynamics of this changing perspective. Historically, the Soviet military used a proactive doctrine to counter external threats. As the perspective changed, the military began looking inward as the old doctrine failed to apply to the new threat. As a result, the military assumed a reactive posture while it waited for new doctrine to be established. The successful transformation of the Russian state in the next few years depends partly on the successful formulation and implementation of a new doctrine. This new doctrine must enable the military to resume a more proactive role in countering the threat posed by local wars.

II

The global superpower perspective is well documented in the Cold War literature. Until the mid- 1980s, Soviet foreign policy and military doctrine evolved to encompass a twofold mission: "open-ended competition with the United States for the spheres of influence in the Third World and containment of China in Asia."[67] A multitude of other secondary missions can also be listed, however, they generally fall under and support the broader category of offensive Cold War superpower competition.

As noted in Chapter Two, the invasion of Afghanistan was viewed as part of the Cold War competition in international relations. The Soviet military performance, however, clearly revealed that the force organized and deployed under a Cold War doctrine would not prevail against an insurgent enemy. Internally, the Afghan failure combined with Russian economic realities compelled the leadership to reevaluate the existing military doctrine. The only way to reshape the internal order and preserve the nation was to reduce the external threat.

The means of reducing the external threat emerged in 1987 when Gorbachev opted to change the national military perspective. On 29 May, during a meeting of the Political Consultative Committee of the Warsaw Pact, with Gorbachev in attendance, a fundamental change was announced. For the first time in history, the Warsaw Pact nations espoused a defensive doctrine. The Soviet MOD, General Dmitry T. Yazov, further explained this doctrine by asserting "...that our military doctrine today consists of a system of basic views on the prevention of war, on military organizational development, preparation of the country and its armed forces for repelling aggression..."[68]

In essence, Gorbachev imposed an unprecedented change to military doctrine based on political and economic necessities rather than historical ideological objectives. The new defensive doctrine provided Gorbachev with the means to enhance a more stable international environment with reduced Cold War tensions. Only in this environment could the massive domestic restructuring program have a chance of succeeding. The political leadership attempted to change the long-term military perspective in order to achieve short-term economic improvement. The new defensive doctrine created significant unexpected repercussions within the military.

In many ways, this shift created an untenable dichotomy between the old and the new. It was a dilemma based "...in the philosophical and doctrinal inability of the traditional Soviet military to accept key principles of Gorbachev's New Thinking."[69] Soviet military leaders were not comfortable with a new doctrine that was defensively based on a concept of national security interests. Unlike their Western democratic counterparts, the military was unable to create a viable conception of national security because "...in the USSR such a conception did not, and was not able to exist, for the Soviet Union as a state was constructed around an ideology and a party as the means of power..."[70] As the military was forced to emerge from the past and unable to conceive the future, its decline began to accelerate.

By 1991, the effect of this dichotomy was evident. Once considered second only to the U.S., the Russian military establishment was a mere shadow of its former self The Russian military was no longer acting in concert with the government in order to preserve the state against domestic disintegration. At this point, the Russian military had clearly lost its global superpower perspective. The reactive institutional and national self preservation perspective began to define military doctrine in the new Russian state.

III

The institutional preservation perspective is resident in the civil-military interaction process and was addressed in the previous chapter. The formulation of military doctrine in relation to new national security concerns has proved to be very difficult. Ethnic considerations, domestic use of force policies, a dynamic political atmosphere and relations with the breakaway republics of the FSU combine to inhibit the formulation of a meaningful military doctrine that will facilitate the national transformation. The doctrine that has emerged focuses on emotional regional challenges that tend to divide, rather than unite the public, political and military opinions.

Ethnic considerations have been a central focus in the formulation of new military doctrine. The protection of ethnic Russians in the "near abroad" provides numerous sources of potential conflicts for the future. The "Provisions of the Military Doctrine of the Russian Federation" clearly identified that "the suppression of rights, freedoms and legitimate interests of citizens of the Russian Federation in foreign states..." constitutes a source of external danger that may require the use of force.[71] Even though the overall tone of the doctrine is defensive in nature, Russia regards the "near abroad" and the Russian citizens as an integral part of its legal sphere of influence. In one sense, the purpose of the military doctrine was misplaced. It has been used as a means of sending a warning message to the former republics rather than providing a positive, constructive role for the future. It is only a matter of time until one of the former republics challenges legitimacy of this doctrine.

Even though the external use of force is very likely in the future, this analysis suggests that the internal use of force is the most dangerous threat to the future of the Russian state. As a result of the 1993 coup attempt, the new military doctrine expands the internal use of military forces. The Russian military is explicitly mandated to suppress

> ...illegal activity by nationalists, separatists, or other organizations which is aimed at destabilizing the situation in the Russian Federation or violating its territorial integrity and which is carried out using armed violence; attempts to overthrow the constitutional system by force or to disrupt the functioning of organs of state power and administration.[72]

As long as the Russian President uses constitutional procedures (unlike in Chechnya), this doctrine can enhance national security. It is the wider range of activities, however, that provides for potential crises in the future. The military doctrine also includes contraband activity, organized crime and narcotics trafficking as internal threats that justify the use of Russian military forces. The use of the military against criminal elements is significant for two key reasons. First, it potentially elevates the Chechen situation back into the realm of military confrontation. One of several sources reports that "Chechens have gained a popular reputation within the former Soviet Union...as among the most cohesive, violent and effective of the ethnic criminal groups....Chechens are particularly active in anus trafficking."[73] By including law enforcement functions within the jurisdiction of the military, the new doctrine opens a wide range of future domestic LIC engagements.

The second problem with this aspect of the military doctrine concerns the criminalization of the military institution. The decline of the Russian military has created (in some areas) a "Mafia in uniform... [where] burgeoning criminal activities by the Russian

Armed Forces...are well on their way to becoming institutionalized."[74] The increasing scope

of this problem has potentially explosive consequences. Not only are individual military

members involved in widespread criminal activity, the problem also includes *groups* within

the armed forces. It has been reported that by mid-1995 Russian military forces were

> ...deeply immersed in criminal activities conducted for personal and group profit.
> Smuggling crimes of all types (particularly drug and arms trafficking), the massive
> diversion of equipment and...criminal violence, all fall under the umbrella of
> organized crime. So do more sophisticated military financial crimes and schemes
> involving a spectrum of banks and financial organizations...and overseas money-
> laundering schemes that in the past would more readily be associated with Latin
> American drug cartels than with a military establishment.[75]

By encompassing criminal aspects, the current military doctrine may actually be setting the

stage for limited conflicts between various groups within the Russian military.

IV

This analysis originally pursued the study of Russian military doctrine in an attempt

to determine its effect on the national self-preservation perspective relative to the LIC

environment. Unfortunately, there is little available on current Russian military doctrine.

Even with the new openness in Russian society, much of this doctrine is still classified or

unavailable. This area of study reveals a two to four year lag in the current literature. The

significance of this doctrine and its effects on the domestic use of force presents a significant

area for ongoing research. Even with these limitations, this study can still derive several

conclusions concerning the military doctrine.

1. Presently, the Russian military doctrine (as well as many other facets of the new

Russian democracy) is not pro-actively changing to meet the needs of the new state. As information concerning the doctrine is obtained, it should be analyzed in terms of its ability to provide the military with a more proactive and positive role in the transformation process.

2. The current military doctrine serves to increase the potential for LIC between Russia and neighboring states, between the military and Russian citizens, and between groups within the military. Some aspects of the doctrine are actually counterproductive to the transformation process.

3. Given the current trend in Russian civil-military relations, any sudden change to Russian military doctrine should be analyzed first in terms of its political expediency rather than military proficiency in order to determine its permanent value.

Chapter 5: LIC And The Future Of The Transformation

> What we anticipate seldom occurs; What we least expect generally happens.
>
> Benjamin Disraeli

I

The Russian future no longer seems to hold the same promise that was envisioned just a few years ago. The new democracy appears to have little chance of successfully completing the transformation in a peaceful manner. The invasion of Afghanistan was the beginning of the Russian transformation. The formal disintegration of the empire in December 1991, marked a distinct separation of two phases within the larger transformation process. The fact that this phase continues to this day raises pertinent questions: Will another phase occur and what would precipitate the transition to another phase? If so, when will it take place and what path will it take? Will it be violent and will it include other European or Asian nations? When will the world (or Russia) know that the transformation has been completed? An attempt to predict Russia's future is neither prudent, possible nor practical. There is information available, however, that allows one to derive general conclusions and make calculated estimates concerning Russia's future and its security.

This chapter analyzes the future of the Russian transformation in light of: the recent military structure and capabilities in relation to the resource base; potential catalysts for the next LIC engagement based on the current situation; and, an assessment of the potential for either a military coup or a civil war.

Ideally, the structure of a military organization should be designed around a well defined set of desired or required capabilities. These military capabilities are generally refined by the civil-military relations process against the backdrop of resource constraints. The result produces a military structure that retains the capabilities required to meet established doctrinal aims. Until the mid-1980s, the Soviet Union was able to achieve this balance; the military structure was capable of fulfilling the Cold War doctrine. To some degree, the established doctrine shaped the Soviet entry into the LIC environment in Afghanistan. However, as the Afghan War became prolonged, the imbalance between doctrine and the deployed military structure and capabilities became evident.

As the empire disintegrated, the balance between military structure, doctrine, resource constraints and the civil-military relations process was lost. The military was expected to execute the new national preservation doctrine with an old international Cold War force structure. The isolation of the military from both the government and society precluded a meaningful role for the military forces in the transformation of the state. As a result, the LIC environment now tends to shape the military.

The civil-military relations and doctrinal aspects that were previously addressed provide insight into how the Russian military evolved to its present status. While these aspects can provide a solid basis for historical research, their elusive nature limits their effectiveness as a measure for future changes. This analysis uses other standards that can more easily be observed and can be used to evaluate the current and future status of the Russian military--the focus is on the military structure in relation to resource constraints. More specifically, it addresses resource constraints in terms of economics and manpower.

In an attempt to deal with the economic crisis, the government has significantly cut defense spending since 1992. These cuts have affected all aspects of the military. The effect of the economic cuts became readily apparent to the outside world. The first evidence that appeared "...in the summer of 1993 was the decision by the civilian airline, Aeroflot, to cease honoring military transportation requests because of unpaid bills the Defense Ministry had piled up."[76] In 1994, the Finance Ministry only released one-half of the military appropriations. The 1995 draft budget allocated even less money. As a result, "in testimony to the State Duma...Russian Defense Minister Pavel Grachev declared flatly that no army in the world is in as wretched state as Russia's. He warned that if only half the proposed 1995 defense allocation is released...the army will simply collapse."[77] Numerous other reports have continued through 1996 which have even included the stoppage of basic utility services for key military installations. The military's relationship with civilian contractors continues to decay.

The economic picture in relation to Russian military manpower reinforces the overall impression of structural and capability decline. By mid-1995, the military retained approximately 1.4 million men and women in the armed forces, even though it had an authorized end strength of up to 1.9 million. Even with this reduced structure, the government did not have enough money to pay for military salaries, housing or benefits. The significance of this problem is realized when "Defense Minister Grachev is reported to have distributed...cash when he visits Russian officers in the field."[78] Without money to pay the soldiers, the government cannot meet its aim of fielding a balanced all-volunteer force. As a result, the draft remains loosely in effect. It is estimated that less than 50 percent of the draftees ever report for duty. The trend that was first identified in 1993 by Sergi Stepashin, former Chairman of the Parliament's Defense Committee, continues to this day; "...the Russian Army is becoming an all-volunteer army, consisting of officers only."[79] In 1996, the trend continues as many officers continue to stay in the Russian military due to lack of other employment opportunities--even if it means filling vacant enlisted jobs.

Not only is there an imbalance between the officer and enlisted structure, the manpower shortage also varies from service to service. It appears that safeguarding the nuclear inventory has a high priority: most of the Strategic Forces have been maintained at authorized strength with experienced personnel. While this is marginally reassuring from a Western or international perspective, it also serves to magnify the downside from the domestic Russian perspective. The majority of the available military structure is focused on safeguarding weapons that have little relevance to Russia's international stature or new military doctrine, while the military forces that counter the nation's greatest threat--domestic or regional LIC--are sacrificed. The army and the navy are receiving less than 50 percent of the required draftees that they need in order to be combat capable. Until this problem is resolved, the government will only be able to field inexperienced "rag-tag" units in response to domestic threats. Recent events in Chechnya represent the capabilities of Russia's military for the foreseeable future.

The defense economic issue has created several other unintended consequences that further isolate the military from both the government and society. The failure of specific regions within Russia to pay taxes has created significant tensions. In one related incident, Deputy Prime Minister Boris Fyodorov stated that "...Russia' s relations with Tartarstan concerned him more than Russia's relations with Ukraine. He has warned that efforts to withhold revenues were totally unacceptable and would produce major upheavals ahead."[80]

In at least one instance, "1,500 crack airborne troops were hired to provide 'physical security' for tax collectors."[81] Again the government has forced the military to assume a dubious role that detracts from its intended doctrinal capabilities.

The lack of government funding has forced the military to begin finding alternate sources of money. Some military leaders have thrown their support behind conservative factions that are attempting to re-centralize the economy. In this case, that military is actually working against the free market economy transition process. Other means of self-financing by the military includes unauthorized arms sales, black market trade, bank loans and even "agreements with local separatist leaders in regions outside of Russia...[82] Even if the degree of such activity is minimal, the potential implications are grave. A military that offers any amount of its loyalty for sale, or is willing to sell its arms to the highest bidder, is a prelude to disaster. Parts of the Russian military are auctioning away the Cold War structure for personal profit and preservation. At some point, the leftover capabilities may not be able to meet the national security requirements.

III

Most historical conflict analysis seeks to identify a specific reason or catalyst for the initiation of hostilities. In some instances, the catalyst is very clear. In other instances, however, the specific cause of the conflict is subject to continuous debate. In all probability, it is in this latter category that the next Russian LIC engagement will reside. Just as the specific motivations for the Afghan and Chechen invasions are debatable, the motives for the next LIC involvement may likewise be ambiguous. Part of the reason for this phenomenon is the complex interrelationship between numerous potential LIC catalysts. In other words, the next LIC engagement will most likely result from a combination of factors.

In an effort to understand the relationship between the combination of factors, this analysis has identified a theoretical framework that establishes basic categories of future Russian LIC potential. A review of the literature on the current state of Russian affairs produces a litany of potential sources of conflict. The most frequent are resources, ethnic issues, social unrest, politics, crime, religion, border disputes and economic decline. Most potential catalysts can be placed into at least one of three categories: political, social or economic.[83]

In many respects, each of these categories directly reflect one of the transitions that were addressed in the opening chapter. The potential political catalysts focus around the transition from a dictatorship to democracy. These include elections and succession crises, constitutional guarantees and the promises of democracy. The potential social catalysts revolve around the transition from empire to nation state. These include ethnic problems, territorial demarcation, religion and Islamic resurgence, and the isolation of the military from society. The potential economic catalysts are naturally a function of the transition from a controlled economy to a free market economy. These catalysts include resource allocation, organized crime, unemployment and social unrest in response to economic decline and inflation.

This research suggests that the rise of nationalism (at the expense of Soviet ideology and the dictatorship) as the predominant pillar of Russian society places the social catalysts in the forefront of LIC precipitation. The ethnic diversity within Russia continues to create significant problems. In addition, the 25 million ethnic Russians in the "near abroad" have already surfaced as a significant source of conflict. The demarcation of new borders is also a problem. Historical memories of the previous empire may tend to aggravate future relations.

When political leaders or candidates espouse nationalist expansion, the apprehension of neighboring states is increased. In one case, the former vice president, Aleksendr Rutskoy claimed that "the demarcation of borders, and nothing but the demarcation of borders...will define Russia as a power."[84] Any of these social catalysts by themselves, however, may not necessarily be sufficient to create the next LIC.

When the attempted control of these social catalysts contribute to, or combine with economic catalysts, the potential for LIC increases dramatically. In this sense, Chechnya serves as an example for the future. In Chechnya, the ethnic and territorial (social) catalysts combined with the economic catalyst of oil revenues to precipitate a conflict. The real danger of these types of conflicts is that they magnify the social and economic problems that the conflict was trying to eliminate in the first place. This creates a downward spiral that ultimately affects the political realm. This phenomenon acts to enhance the disproportionate effect of LIC within the country.

Further research suggests that a political catalyst (by itself) is least likely to initiate a Russian conflict. As long as the social and economic catalysts are controlled, it is unlikely that a political catalyst will precipitate an internal conflict. There is one area, however, in which the political catalysts might provoke conflict, especially if combined with economic incentives. Any political change within Russia that threatens the promises of democracy, economic well-being or the new freedoms of neighboring states, creates a significant potential for international conflict. An interview with the Ukrainian military exchange officer at the United States Marine COTS Command and Staff College, Major Valeriy Roudenok, reinforced this theme; he continually focused on Russian economics rather than the political aspects as a likely potential catalyst for the next regional conflict.[85]

Even though the Russian transformation may not proceed in a peaceful manner, this does not necessarily mean that it will fail in the near future. Events in Chechnya, at least under the present circumstances, reveals that Russia can withstand the effects of a LIC engagement. In the near term, limited LIC involvement which is precipitated by social (and even limited economic) catalysts may not halt the transformation. There is a high degree of probability that future limited LIC (in the next two to three years) will only slow the three transitions, but the overall transformation process will continue. There are, however, other scenarios that might halt the transformation: a military coup or a full civil war.

This analysis did not focus on the potential conduct or outcome of a full civil war. While there is certainly a Russian historical precedent for such an event, it would most likely be proceeded by a prolonged period of increased LIC activity. In addition, the civil war aspect falls outside of the LIC realm. The purpose of this analysis is merely to identify the potential LIC aspects that may serve as a prelude to wider conflict.

A coup attempt by the military would signify a dramatic shift in the dynamics of the Russian trinity. In effect, it would symbolize the end of the military's willingness to foster the transition from dictatorship to democracy. The military would assume an active and dominant role in the political process. As previously indicated, a political catalyst appears least likely to initiate the next LIC engagement. The military's desire to remain outside of politics serves to reinforce the small probability of a military coup.

There are other factors indicating the military's inability to stage a successful coup. First, Chechnya illustrated just how divided and weak the military has become. While a few key military leaders might attempt to seize power "the evidence strongly suggests, however, that few if any military units would respond...because there is no broad-based allegiance within the military today."[86] In addition, a coup in a country the size of Russia would require a vast military effort that is beyond current military capability. Thus far, the military has declined to intervene directly on two previous occasions (1991 and 1993). In those instances, the military was more powerful and united than it is today.

Recently, many observers have noted retired General Alexander Lebed's increasing popularity and his presidential ambitions. Much of Lebed's popularity resulted from his ability to obtain a Chechen peace accord. His political power base is derived from reducing military activity, not increasing it. A recent poll taken among the officer corps concerning the level of military professionalism in the senior officer ranks revealed that Lebed fared no better than Defense Minister Grachev.[87] None of the highest military leaders retain enough support from either society or the military to assume direct political control. If a military leader assumes political power in the near future, it will most likely be the result of the democratic process.

Even though a political catalyst (to include a military coup) is least likely to precipitate future LIC involvement, this scenario is the most dangerous. While Russia might be able to "muddle through" another LIC engagement similar to Chechnya, the same cannot be said should the military enter the political arena. A dynamic political shift that attempts to reinvigorate the military will also have a dramatic effect on the economy. International Monetary Fund appropriations and capital investment would quickly disappear. Should this scenario occur, a full scale civil war would most likely follow.

The world will certainly know when (or if) the Russian transformation fails--the costs of prolonged LIC and wider regional conflict will regain predominance in the world's attention span. On the other hand, it will be difficult for the world to recognize the successful completion of the transformation. It must be emphasized that "since the past is still very much in place," this transformation process may require a decade or more to achieve success. This analysis offers several conclusions that can be used to identify Russian success. First, the democratic process must become institutionalized. The Russian people must begin to believe and trust in the ability of democracy to ensure the peaceful transfer of political power. Democracy and freedom must assume at least a coequal status with nationalism as one of the pillars of society.

Second, the military must find its proper role both within the new nation state and among its new neighbors. The last vestiges of the imperial military establishment must be eliminated. If the Russian military structure, capabilities, doctrine, resource allocation and civil-military relations are balanced, the transformation will be in a healthy state. One other means of identifying Russian success is somewhat ironic. When the West again recognizes the potential power of a well trained and equipped Russian military force, the transformation will be close to completion.

Finally, and probably most important to the entire process, is the growth of the Russian economy. Any reduction in the rate of GNP decline will be a positive indicator. Actual GNP growth and enhanced international trade with Russia's new neighbors are other signs of a successful transformation. While numerous economic indicators can reveal success, the most important factor relates to the economy's positive impact on society. A prosperous, efficient economy that provides goods and services beyond that of the old Soviet economy is one of the surest signs of success. Positive economic results will cause the people to look to the future rather than the past.

Chapter 6: Russian LIC And Global Implications For The 21st Century

> That which stops growing begins to rot.
> Minister to Catherine the Great, late 18th century.

I

In Chapter One, the two major purposes of this research were identified. The primary purpose was to raise the level of awareness concerning major conflict potential on the Eurasian continent as a result of a Russian LIC catalyst. This purpose was derived directly from the thesis statement--a LIC catalyst will precipitate the next Russian Revolution which has the potential to spread into a global or at least a multinational Eurasian conflict. The second purpose was to raise new questions concerning the role of LIC in the new world order. This purpose was derived from an intent to foster the application of Russia's LIC lessons to the wider global community. Combined, these two purposes might provide a greater professional understanding of the detrimental effect of prolonged LIC engagements as the 21st Century approaches.

This chapter summarizes prolonged LIC effects in relation to the Russian trinity and the global powers in the new world order. It also briefly addresses Russia's future and the measures that might prevent a repetition of history.

II

Russia is a vastly different country today as compared to December, 1979 when the first Soviet troops entered Afghanistan. During the past 17 years, phenomenal changes have occurred throughout Russia. It is also important to remember that Russian military forces have been engaged in LIC combat for 12 of the 17 years. This prolonged LIC involvement has been an integral part of these dynamic changes--the Russian trinity will never be the same.

Of the three parts of the trinity, the Russian people have been most affected by the prolonged LIC experiences. While the Afghanistan and Chechen LIC experiences have many similarities, the two conflicts appear to have played significantly different roles in the civil transformation process. On one hand, the end of the Afghan War was part of the *perestroika* era of openness. In a sense, the withdrawal from Afghanistan was part of a new future that was full of promise. In just a few short years, however, Chechnya (and the concurrent economic decline) served to remind the people that "the past is still very much in place."[88] Regardless of the lack of public support, Russian leaders were determined to commit troops for an extended period of time. A recent article summarizes the evolution of Russian society by explaining that,

> The very foundations of civil society are weak because Russians, despite their new freedoms, have become extraordinarily passive. They are not in the mood to participate. They are puzzled, distrustful, uncertain and preoccupied with personal survival. Although there was an outpouring of spontaneous support--mass street demonstrations--in the years of *perestroika*...now Russians appear to be disappointed and looking inward, just at the time when civil society is being born.[89]

Research suggests that the experience in Chechnya magnified the feelings of puzzlement, distrust, uncertainty and disappointment. Public opinion poll data taken from before and after the initial Chechen invasion (1993 and 1995) is revealing:

The modification (although some would define it as the creation) of a Russian civil

society is an extremely difficult task given the centuries of authoritarian and totalitarian

tradition. The invasion of Chechnya compounded the problems facing this Russian transition.

Although the survey data does not attempt to isolate the specific cause of the negative

opinion shift, the specific cause may be unimportant. A prolonged LIC engagement will

magnify any weaknesses that already exist within a society. In Russia, the effects of LIC are

potentially catastrophic since it tends to magnify public apathy. The potential consequences

were revealed in a commentary of the survey data. It stated that "if they manage to build a

working civil society, Russians may remain committed to the democratic path, but without it

they risk drifting back to authoritarianism."[91]

While the people are the most affected by LIC, it is normally the government that has

the most control over LIC participation. One result of the Russian LIC experiences has been

the complete transformation of the political perspective in regard to the use of force. The

invasion of Afghanistan was an offensive military means to expand Soviet influence. The

political leadership perceived a choice and they chose to invade in order to capitalize on an

opportunity. Chechnya, however, was different--a choice no longer existed. The political

leadership felt compelled or forced to invade. Again, the specific causes of the invasion are less important. Whether or not the invasion was designed to preserve Russian integrity or to preserve personal political power is irrelevant. What really matters is the perspective. Chechnya represented a loss of political control and the only available response was the use of force.

Compounding the political perspective problem is the failure to learn from past mistakes. In both Afghanistan and Chechnya, Russian leaders continued to prosecute LIC engagements while simultaneously coping with leadership health problems or succession crises. In addition, the apparent absence of constraints and historical misapplications worked to the detriment of political decision making in the LIC environment.

If the government perceives little choice and repeats mistakes, the LIC effects will be magnified in two ways. First, the decision to use force will more readily be made. Second, the mistakes will tend to prolong the conflict. Current Russian leaders must guard against these pitfalls to ensure that a prolonged war weariness does not make possible another October Revolution.

Some would argue that the Russian military--not the people--have been most affected by the recent conflicts. While there is some merit to that view, this research offers a different perspective. There is little disagreement that the Russian military is in complete disarray. One must ask, however, is the current status of the Russian military a direct result of the LIC involvement. In terms of casualties and hardware, the LIC involvement expended relatively few military resources. The military's demise is not consistent with historical examples of similar great powers which suffered destruction and defeat on the battlefield. The remnants of the former Soviet Army still retain a tremendous latent potential. Consider the result if all the states of the FSU were attacked by an outside force. This outside force would face a substantial military obstacle in the form a reunifying army. In other words, Soviet military power was largely fragmented, dispersed and isolated--it was not destroyed.

This perspective is amplified when the fragmentation of the Russian military (vice the entire Soviet military) is examined further. Not only was the Russian military externally fragmented as the Soviet Union broke apart, it was also fragmented internally. Without an ideology to preserve, the traditional civil-military relationship was left without a foundation. In addition, as society focused on freedom and economic prosperity, the military became further isolated from the society and the government. This dual fragmentation (internal and external) reveals the true destructive force of prolonged LIC. Even though the military is not destroyed on the battlefield, LIC has the potential to render an army ineffective by other means.

In a prolonged LIC environment, the people are most directly affected, but the military bears the burden of dealing with disproportionate and asymmetrical effects of the battles. The latent potential of the fragmented and isolated military creates the potential for a devastating catalyst. As the Russian society and government forge a new path into the 21st century, the military represents a source of power that could halt the transformation process. If the military solidifies its fragmented structure before it is provided with a new national security role, a successful military coup is within the realm of possibility. By attempting to use the military in another unpopular LIC engagement, the government might actually increase popular support for a larger military role in the affairs of the state. As the 21st century approaches, Russia's challenge is to re-balance the trinity. This can best be achieved through economic strength and by avoiding the disproportionate effects of prolonged LIC.

As stated in Chapter One, the ability to move from a controlled economy to a successful free market economy is Russia's greatest hurdle. Continued economic decline provides a fertile ground for future LIC within Russia or with one of its new neighbors. A poor economy will magnify any one of a number of other factors that might otherwise remain dormant. This combination of factors creates a very real possibility of igniting a LIC catalyst that has the potential to affect much of Europe and the world for years to come.

III

As the 20th century concludes, global leaders must reflect on the century's lessons in order to prepare for the new millennium. This reflection will reveal that the past 100 years has been the harbinger of unprecedented change--especially in the character of warfare. The reflection should also reveal that future choices are very similar to choices already made in the 20th century. This dichotomy between a rapidly evolving past and the similarities of the future provides the most important challenge to the leadership of the 21st century. Global leaders must accurately cull and understand the lessons from the past and more importantly, they must correctly apply them to future situations.

In the 21st century, the stakes in the LIC arena will most likely be higher than they are today. Few, if any, countries can afford to selectively apply history to fit their needs in the LIC environment. For those who have the wisdom to recognize it, Russia has provided the world with a valuable lesson. The Russian LIC experiences (and the U.S. experience in Vietnam) demonstrate that the impact of a LIC failure on a global power will be disproportionately magnified in relation to the military losses. In the future, nations must assess the significance of their LIC involvement in relation to the domestic impact on the government, the society, the military institution and the economy. An attempt to measure the impact of LIC solely in terms of the battlefield is not only irrelevant, it becomes detrimental to the nation. In the 20th century, the tendency for leaders to initially focus on the battlefield costs, rather than the domestic costs, allowed the conflicts to become prolonged. The global powers cannot afford to lose focus in the future.

This lesson has two specific applications in the new world order. The primary lesson pertains to the relationship between the economy and LIC. A requirement exists for a fundamental understanding that a solid economic foundation is one of the most effective means of deterring LIC. A viable and prosperous economy that provides a reasonable distribution of wealth can minimize other factors that have the potential to become a LIC catalyst.

The second application pertains to the military, however, it is closely tied to the economic foundation. In the new world order, global powers must be proactive in maintaining the balance between military structure, capabilities, doctrine, civil-military relations and resource constraints. An attempt to maintain either an obsolete or excessive armed force will detract from the economic base. Military forces in the next century must be efficiently organized in order to deter, or at least minimize the effects of LIC. Much of the military efficiency rests with the political leadership. The civil-military relationships must provide the military with a proper role in the trinity. At the same time, the leadership must appropriately balance and shape military doctrine within the bounds of supportable structure and resource constraints. In the 21st century, a military organization that is inefficient, unbalanced, fragmented or isolated from the government or society will be increasingly susceptible to the effects of LIC.

Does history really repeat itself? This question creates endless debate that, in the end resolves very little. A more pertinent question should be asked. How can history be used to prevent a repetition of past mistakes? The answer lies in the ability to recognize similar trends and then correctly correlate the past with the present in order to prevent the repetition of mistakes. Chart #1 (next page) provides a means to recognize similar historical Russian trends. The top portion of the chart graphically portrays the first two paragraphs of the chronology presented in Chapter One. The focus of this analysis is reflected on the bottom portion of the chart. This includes the LIC events that comprise catalyst #1 between 1979 and 1996 and the potential circumstances that might precipitate catalyst #2 as Russia enters the 21st century. Similar trends between the past and the present are easily identified.

In light of the similarities, this analysis concludes by suggesting two means that may prevent the repetition of Russian history. First, all parts of the Russian trinity must recognize that the current instability has the potential to rapidly become a larger Eurasian conflict. Only by honestly working to institutionalize democracy can the Russians avoid the pitfalls of a past which is still very much in place. The transition from a dictatorship to a democracy is essential.

The transition from an empire to a nation state will also enhance the prospects for a bright future in the 21st century. As potential LIC catalysts arise, the resolution of these conflicts and the use of force cannot subvert the growth and acceptance of the democratic process. Russian leaders must revise their relationships with many parts of the old empire. This revision applies especially to Chechnya and other ethnically diverse populations. For the greater good of the new Russian State, these revised relationships may require greater

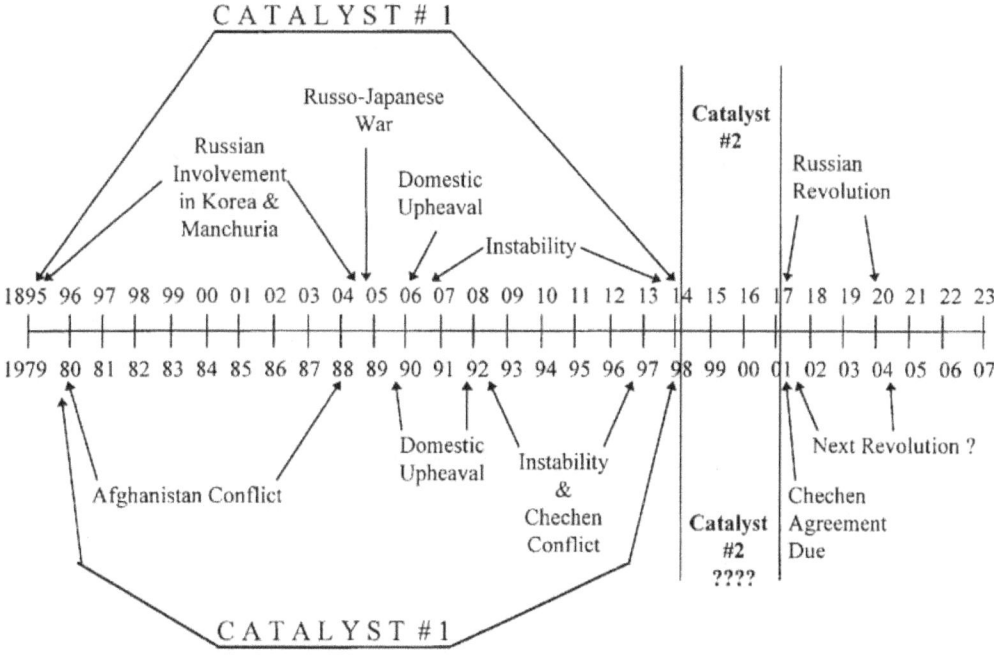

freedoms or *even independence for some regions.* Russian leaders must change their

perspective. They should not be asking how they can force regions to support the

transformation--this represents imperial thinking of the past. They must start asking what the

state can do to for these regions and peacefully encourage their support of the transformation.

Both of these means must be enhanced by the success of a free market economy.

Overall success requires a disciplined and determined look to the future. For a society

that is held captive by its past, this creates a very uncomfortable feeling. Russia can only

grow by facing this uncomfortable break with its past and learning from its mistakes. Russian

leaders must remember the advice given to Catherine the Great over 200 years ago-that

which stops growing begins to rot. The advice is still very applicable today. A failure to heed

this advice will precipitate a LIC catalyst that will affect Europe, Asia and much of the world

well into the 21st Century--history will repeat itself

NOTES

[1] Ernest Dupuy and Trevor N. Dupuy, *The Encyclopedia of Military History from 3500 B.C. to the Present* (New York: Harper and Row, Publishers, 1986), 930.

[2] Carl Von Clausewitz, *On War,* translated and edited by Michael Howard and Peter Paret (Princeton, NJ: Princeton University Press, 1984), 89.

[3] Daniel Yergin and Thane Gustafson, *Russia 2010 and What it Means for the World* (New York: Vintage Books, 1995), 4. Emphasis of the last sentence added. This idea serves as a recurring theme throughout this analysis.

[4] Ibid,4.

[5] David T. Twining, The New Eurasia: A Guide to the Republics of the Former Soviet Union (Westport, CT: Praeger Publishers, 1993), 23.

[6] Ibid., 7.

[7] Ibid., 12.

[8] Paul Kennedy, *The Rise and Fall of the Great Powers: Economic Change and Military Conflict from 1500 to 2000* (New York: Vintage Books, 1989), 489-490.

[9] Ibid., 513.

[10] Ibid., 513.

[11] Twining, 5.

[12] Yergin, 6.

[13] Kennedy, 514.

[14] The discussion on defensive motivations to include the Brezhnev Doctrine, Islamic resurgence and the traditional fear of encirclement is important, however, specific analysis is beyond the scope of this research.

[15] Ibid., 135.

[16] Robert Jervis, *Perception and Misperception in International Relations* (Princeton, NJ: Princeton University Press, 1986), 278.

[17] Lester W. Grau, (tans. and ed.). *The Bear Went Over the Mountain: Soviet Combat Tactics in Afghanistan.* Washington, D.C.: National Defense University Press, 1996, xiv.

[18] Ibid., xii.

[19] Mohammad Y. Nawroz and Lester W. Grau, *The Soviet War in Afghanistan: History and Harbinger of Future War?* U.S. Army, Foreign Military Studies Office, Ft. Leavenworth, KS. Downloaded from *America On-Line* on 3 November 1996, 7.

[20] Bernard Gwertzman and Michael T. Kaufman, (eds.), *The Decline and Fall of the Soviet Empire* (New York, NY: The New York Times Company, 1992), 102.

[21] Grau, 201.

[22] Ibid., 201.

[23] Nawroz, 4.

[24] Ibid., 4.

[25] Ibid., 4.

[26] This book was written at the Frunze Military Academy by Russian military leaders with combat experience for the primary purpose of passing on the lessons learned in Afghanistan.

[27] Gwertzman and Kaufman, ix.

[28] Ibid., ix.

[29] Timothy L. Thomas, *The Caucasus Conflict and Russian Security: The Russian Armed Forces Confront Chechnya* (U.S. Army, Foreign Military Studies Office, Ft. Leavenworth, KS: January, 1995), 6. Downloaded from *America On-Line* on 3 November 1996.

[30] John Colarusso, "Chechnya: A War Without Winners." *Current History* 94, no. 594 (October 1995): 330.

[31] Thomas, 6.

[32] Michael McFaul, "Eurasia Letter: Russian Politics After Chechnya." *Foreign Policy,* no. 99 (Summer 1995): 153.

[33] Calorusso, 333.

[36] Ibid., 333.

[35] Thomas, 5.

[38] Ibid., 5.

[39] *Facts on File,* 1996, 646. This source openly acknowledges that these figures may be inflated by Lebed in order to foster his agenda in the region. The number of casualties ranges very widely and this source does represent the highest figures found in this research effort to date.

[40] David Isby, *War in a Distant Country Afghanistan: Invasion and Resistance,* (London, UK: Arms and Armour Press, 1989), 62. The per year data is based on 10 years of involvement.

[41] Facts on File, 1997, 50. The per year data is based on two years of involvement.

[42] McFaul, 157.

[43] Reuters News Service, "Chernomydin Says Chechnya Must Stay in Russia." 8 October 1996. Downloaded from *America On-Line* on 21 November 1996.

[44] McFaul, 165. The author of this quote wrote this passage in reference to the 1996 elections, but it is even more applicable to the year 2000 election given the unresolved Chechen situation.

[45] Vera Tolz, "Moscow and Russia's Ethnic Republics in the Wake of Chechnya." *Post Soviet Prospects* 3, no. 10 (October 1995). Downloaded from America On-Line on 14 October 1996. 3.

[46] Ibid., 4.

[47] Ibid., 4. Taken from original source: Interfax, 20 January 1995.

[48] Stephen J. Blank and Earl Tilford, Jr., "Russia's Invasion of Chechnya: A Preliminary Assessment." *Strategic Studies Institute,* Special Report, U.S. Army War College, 13.

[49] Reference to the introductory quotes of this chapter.

[50] Timothy I Colton and Thane Gustafson (eds.), *Soldiers and the Soviet State: Civil-Military Relations from Brezhnev to Gorbachev* (Princeton, NJ: Princeton University Press, 1990), 285.

[51] Dale R. Herspring and Ivan Volgyes, (eds.), *Civil-Military Relations in Communist Systems* (Boulder, CO: Westview Press, 1978), 92.

[52] The removal of Marshal Ogarkov, Chief of the Soviet General Staff, in 1984 was another example. He was abruptly transferred when he openly challenged the Minister of Defense on d6tente, military budgets and national security decision making. This incident may be interpreted as an intra-military affair rather than a civil-military affair. Nonetheless, it served as a warning to other high ranking military leaders.

[53] Colton and Gustafson, 286.

[54] Ibid., 287.

[55] Ibid., 318.

[56] Timothy J. Colton, and Robert Legvold (eds.), *After the Soviet Union: From Empire to Nations* (New York, NY: W. W. Norton and Company, 1992), 118.

[57] Ibid., 118-9.

[58] Gwertzman, 431. Ironically, this is roughly the same percentage that was removed by Stalin's purges in 1937-8.

[59] Colton and Levgold, 119.

[60] Yergin, 87.

[61] James F., Holcomb, and Michael M. Boll. "Russia's New Doctrine: Two Views." *Strategic Studies Institute,* U.S. Army War College, 1994 , 25.

[62] Ibid., 1-2.

[63] Blank, 5.

[64] Ibid., 8.

[65] Jacob Kipp and Timothy L. Thomas, *The Russian Military and the 1995 Parliamentary Elections: A Primer.* U.S. Army, Foreign Military Studies Office, Ft. Leavenworth, KS.: (5 October 1995). Downloaded from *America On-Line* on 3 November 1996.

[66] Ibid., 2.

[67] Teresa P. Johnson, and Steven E. Miller (eds.), *Russian Security After the Cold War. Seven Views From Moscow* (Cambridge, MA: Center for Science and International Affairs, John F. Kennedy School of Government, Harvard University, 1994), 3.

[68] Willard C. Frank, Jr. and Philips S. Gillette, (eds.), Soviet Military Doctrine from Lenin to Gorbachev, 19 15-1991 (Westport, CT: Greenwood Press, 1992), 41.

[69] Holcomb and Boll, 15.

[70] Ibid., 17.

[71] Ibid., 3.

[72] Ibid., 6.

[73] Graham H. Turbiville, Jr., "The Chechen Ethno-Religious Conflict, Terrorism and Crime." *Military Review* 3, vol. 74, (March 1994): 19.

[74] Graham H. Turbiville, Jr., "Mafia in Uniform: The Criminalization of the Russian Armed Forces," U.S. Army, Foreign Military Studies Office, Ft. Leavenworth, KS: 2. Downloaded from *America On-Line* on 3 November 1996.

[75] Ibid., 6.

[76] Ibid., 88.

[77] Lambeth, 88.

[78] Gustafson, 86-87.

[79] Ibid., 87. In 1993, the Russian Army had somewhere between *1.5* and 1.8 million members with approximately 690,000 officers. In comparison, in 1996 the U.S. military had approximately 1.5 million members, yet it only had about 233,000 officers according to *Defense '96 Almanac.*

[80] Dawaishia and Parrott, 169.

[81] Ibid., 169.

[82] Ibid., 169.

[83] Certainly, some of these specific catalysts fit into more than one category. An attempt to further subdivide or categorize these catalysts is beyond the scope of this work, yet it does provide another opportunity for additional research.

[84] Dawisha and Parrott, 34.

[85] Major Valeriy Roudenok, Ukrainian military exchange officer at the USMC Command and Staff College, interview by author, 25 October 1996.

[86] Meyer, 327.

[87] Ibid., 327.

[88] Yergin and Gustafson, 4.

[89] David Hoffman, "History of State Power Stymies Growth of Russian Civil Society," The Washington Post, 26 December 1996, A40.

[90] Ibid., A40. *The Washington Post* credited the original source: "Support for Democratic and Political Opposition in Russia, 1993 - 1995," Stephen Whitefield and Geoffrey Evans, Post-Soviet Affairs, Vol. 12, No. 3, July-Sept 1996. The results were drawn from two surveys of Russian population in 1993 and 1995.

[91] Ibid., A40.

BIBLIOGRAPHY

Alford, Jonathon, ed. *The Soviet Union. Security Policies and Constraints.* New York, NY: St. Martin's Press, 1985.

Avidar,Yosef. *The Party and the Army in the Soviet Union.* University Park, PA: The Pennsylvania State University Press, 1983.
.

Blank, Stephen J. and Earl Tilford, Jr. "Does Russian Democracy Have a Future?." *Strategic Studies Institute,* Special Report, U.S. Army War College, 1994.

Blank, Stephen J. and Earl Tilford, Jr. "Russia's Invasion of Chechnya: A Preliminary Assessment." *Strategic Studies Institute,* Special Report, U.S. Army War College,

Celestan, Gregory J. *Wounded Bear: The Ongoing Russian Military Operation in Chechnya.* U.S. Army, Foreign Military Studies Office, Ft. Leavenworth, KS., (August 1996). Downloaded from *America On-Line* on 3 November 1996.

"Chechnya Political Talks Delayed." *Facts on File* 56, 5 September, 1996, p. 632.

"Chernomydin Says Chechnya Must Stay in Russia." Reuters News Service, 8 October 1996. Downloaded from *America On Line* on 21 November 1996.

Church, George J. "Rebellion in Russia." *Time,* 26 December 1994, 116-119+.

Clausewitz, Carl Von. *On War.* Edited and translated by Michael Howard and Peter Paret. Princeton, NJ: Princeton University Press, 1984.

Colarusso, John. "Chechnya: The War Without Winners." *Current History* 94, no 594 (October 1995): 329-336.

Collins, Joseph J. *The Soviet Invasion of Afghanistan: A Study in the Use of Force in Soviet Foreign Policy.* Lexington, MA: Lexington Books, 1986.

Colton, Timothy J. *Commissars, Commanders, and Civilian Authority: The Structure of Soviet Military Politics.* Cambridge, MA: Harvard University Press, 1979.

Colton,Timothy J. and Thane Gustafson, eds. *Soldiers and the Soviet State: Civil-Military Relations from Brezhnev to Gorbachev.* Princeton, NJ: Princeton University Press, 1990.

Colton, Timothy J. and Robert Legvold, eds. *After the Soviet Union: From Empire to Nations.* New York, NY: W. W. Norton and Company, 1992.

Dawisha, Karen and Bruce Parrott *Russia and the New States of Eurasia: The Politics of Upheaval.* New York, NY: Cambridge University Press, 1994.

Dupuy, R. Ernest and Trevor N. Dupuy. *The Encyclopedia of Military History from 3500 B. C. to the Present.* New York, NY: Harper and Row, Publishers, 1986.

Fitzgerald, Mary C. *The New Revolution in Russian Military Affairs.* London: Royal United Services Institute for Defence Studies. 1994.

Foye, Stephen. CNN Interview downloaded from *America On-Line* on 19 November 1996.

Frank, Willard C., Jr. and Philip S. Gillette, (eds). *Soviet Military Doctrine from Lenin to Gorbachev, 1915-1 991.* Westport. CT: Greenwood Press, 1992.

Galeotti, Mark. "Decline and Fall -- Budennovsk and the Chechen War." *Jane ~ Intelligence Review 7,* no. 8: 338.

Galeotti, Mark. "Decline and Fall -- Moscow's Chechen War." *Jane 's Intelligence Review* 7, no. 2 (DATE): 338.

Geibel, Adam. "Lessons in Urban Combat: Grozny, New Year's Eve, 1994." *Infantry* 85, no. 6 (November-December 1995): 21-25.

Geibel, Adam. "Caucasus Nightmare--Red Dawn in Chechnya: A Campaign Chronicle." *Armor* 104, no. 2 (March-April *95): 10-15.*

Grau, Lester W. (trans. and ed.). *The Bear Went Over the Mountain. Soviet Combat Tactics in Afghanistan.* Washington, D.C.: National Defense University Press, 1996.

Gwertzman, Bernard and Michael T. Kaufman, eds. *The Decline and Fall of the Soviet Empire.* New York, NY: The New York Times Company, 1992.

Herspring, Dale R. and Ivan Volgyes, (ed.). *Civil-Military Relations in Communist Systems.* Boulder, CO: Westview Press, 1978.

Hoffman, David. "History of State Power Stymies Growth of Russian Civil Society," *The Washington Post,* 26 December 1996, A40.

Holcomb, James F., and Michael M. Boll. "Russia's New Doctrine: Two Views." *Strategic Studies Institute,* U.S. Army War College, 1994.

Holden, Gerard. *Russia After the Cold War: The Nation in Post-Soviet Security Politics.* Bolder, CO: Westview Press 1994.

International Institute for Strategic Studies, *The Military Balance 1990-1991.* London, UK: Brassey's, 1990.

International Institute for Strategic Studies, *The Military Balance 1994-1995.* London, UK: Brassey's, 1994.

Isby, David. *War In A Distant Country Afghanistan: Invasion and Resistence.* London, UK: Arms and Armour Press, 1989.

Jervis, Robert. *Perception and Misperception in International Relations.* Princeton, NJ: Princeton University Press, 1976.

Johnson, Teresa P. and Steven E. Miller, eds. *Russian Security After the Cold War. Seven Views From Moscow.* Cambridge, MA: Center for Science and International Affairs, John F. Kennedy School of Government, Harvard University, 1994.

Jones, Ellen. *Red Army and Society. A Sociology of the Soviet Military.* Boston: Allen and Unwin, 1985.

Kennedy, Paul. *The Rise and Fall of the Great Powers: Economic Change and Military Conflict from 1500 to 2000.* New York, NY: Vintage Books, 1989.

Kipp, Jacob and Timothy L. Thomas. *The Russian Military and the 1995 Parlimentary Elections. A Primer.* U.S. Army, Foreign Military Studies Office, Ft. Leavenworth, KS., (5 October 1995). Downloaded from *America On-Line* on *3 November 1996.*

Lambeth, Benjamin S. "Russia's Wounded Military." *Foreign Affairs* 74, no. 2 (March-April1995): 86-98.

McFaul, Michael. "Eurasia Letter: Russian Politics After Chechnya." *Foreign Policy,* no. 99 (Summer 1995): 149-165.

Meyer, Stephen M. "The Devolution of Russian Military Power." *Current History* 94, no. 594 (October 1995): 322-328.

Morrison, James W. *Vladimir Zhirinovskiy: An Assessment of a Russian Ultra-Nationalist.* Institute for National Strategic Studies, National Defense University, no 30, Washington, D.C.: April 1994.

Nahaylo, Bohdan, and Victor Swoboda. *Soviet Disunion: A History of the Nationalities Problem in the USSR.* New York, NY: Free Press, 1990.

Nawroz, Mohammad Y. and Lester W. Grau *The Soviet War in Afghanistan: History and Harbinger of Future War?* U.S. Army, Foreign Military Studies Office, Ft. Leavenworth, KS. Downloaded from *America On-Line* on 3 November 1996.

Nelan, Bruce W. "Mr. Yeltsin's Ugly War." *Time,* 29 January 1996, 49.

"Report Charts Out Refugee Flows." Facts on File 56, 13 June 1996, p. 418.

"The Military Mess in Russia." *The Economist* 333, no. 7894 (17 December 1994): 50.

Thomas, Timothy L. *The Caucasus Con and Russian Security: The Russian Armed Forces Confront Chechnya.* U.S. Army, Foreign Military Studies Office, Ft. Leavenworth, KS., (January 1995). Downloaded from *America On-Line* on 3 November 1996.

Tolz, Vera. "Moscow and Russia's Ethnic Republics in the Wake of Chechnya." *Post Soviet Prospects* 3, no. 10 (October 1995). Downloaded from *America On Line,* 14 October 1996.

Tsygankov, V.A., translated by Robert Love. *Using Force of Arms to Provide Domestic Security.* U.S. Army, Foreign Military Studies Office, Ft. Leavenworth, KS, (January 1995). Downloaded from *America On-Line* on 3 November 1996.

Turbiville, Graham H., Jr. "The Chechen Ethno-Religious Conflict, Terrorism and Crime." *Military Review* 3, vol. 74, (March 1994): 19-22.

Turbiville, Graham H., Jr. "Mafia in Uniform: The Criminalization of the Russian Armed Forces." U.S. Army, Foreign Military Studies Office, Ft. Leavenworth, KS. Downloaded from *America On-Line* on 3 November 1996.

Twining, David T. *The New Eurasia. A Guide to the Republics of the Former Soviet Union.* Westport, CT: Praeger Publishers, 1993.

"Why Chechnya Matters." *The Economist* 333, no. 7894 (17 December 1994): 49-51+.

"Yeltsin Orders Last Troops to Withdraw from Chechnya." *Washington Post,* 24 Nov 1996, Sec. A38.

Yergin, Daniel, and Thane Gustafson. *Russia 2010 and What it means for the World.* New York, NY: Vintage Books, 1995.

Yousaf, Mohammad, S. Bt. *Silent Soldier. The Man Behind the Afghan Jehad, General Akhtar Abdur Rahman Shaheed.* Lahore, Pakistan: Jang Publishers 1993.